SHINING ON

SHINING ON

11 star authors' illuminating stories

ROSIE RUSHTON

CELIA REES

ANNE FINE

SUE LIMB

MEG CABOT

LOIS LOWRY

MALORIE BLACKMAN

JACQUELINE WILSON

CATHY HOPKINS

MELVIN BURGESS

MEG ROSOFF

Foreword by Lois Lowry

Delacorte Press

Published by Delacorte Press
an imprint of Random House Children's Books
a division of Random House, Inc.
New York

Delacorte Press and colophon are registered trademarks of Random House, Inc.

1% of profits from the sale of this book will be donated to CureSearch.

www.randomhouse.com/teens

Educators and librarians, for a variety of teaching tools, visit us at
www.randomhouse.com/teachers

Library of Congress Cataloging-in-Publication Data is available upon request.
ISBN: 978-0-385-73472-1 (trade)
ISBN: 978-0-385-90470-4 (lib. binding)

The text of this book is set in 12-point Goudy.
Book design by Kenneth Holcomb

Printed in the United States of America

10 9 8 7 6 5 4 3 2 1

First Edition

CONTENTS

Lois Lowry
FOREWORD vii

Meg Rosoff • Resigned 1

Meg Cabot • Allie Finklestein's Rules
  for Boyfriends .16

Melvin Burgess • Coming Home 32

Anne Fine • Getting the Message 45

Sue Limb • You're a Legend 58

Jacqueline Wilson • The Bad Sister 71

Celia Rees • Calling the Cats 82

Malorie Blackman • Humming Through
  My Fingers 98

Lois Lowry • A Summer to Die 116

Rosie Rushton • Skin Deep 127

Cathy Hopkins • John Lennon Said 139

ABOUT THE AUTHORS 155

FOREWORD

"There's got to be *somewhere* I can be just me," a teenage boy named Gregory shouts at his mother in Anne Fine's story "Getting the Message."

Looking for such a somewhere is a theme in all young people's lives as they mature and try to sort out who they are and where they fit in the world.

When the low blows that are part of every life interfere and mess things up, it is even harder to find the somewhere. That's what the stories in this collection are about: fighting through to find one's place.

It has always been tough to be young.

It is especially tough to be young *today*.

And each of these authors has added another element to that toughness. A physical handicap. A fractured family. A troubling past. A parent who stops being one. A memory that isn't true.

There are always people—usually parents—who want

to protect youngsters, to help them along, to make things easy. It was true for me as a kid; my parents wanted things to be easy and painless for me, and safe, and I fought against them to find my own way of being. Then I did the same thing to my own children, trying to shield them from the hard things. They fought back, of course, as I once had.

These stories are about that, too: about the need young people feel to face their own conflicts; to knock down the protective barrier that their parents have placed around them; to pry open the hidden, undiscussed things and look head-on at what's really there to be battled.

"You can find the roots just under the surface almost anywhere in our garden," the narrator, Laurence, comments in Melvin Burgess's "Coming Home" as he watches his father dig in the yard of the home that is being destroyed by secrets. In "Getting the Message," Gregory insists that his family face the thing they've been avoiding, the question of his sexuality.

These are realistic, contemporary stories. Reading them, I was surprised to come across one that was different. A ghost story! Supernatural beings, rising from graves, taking on new forms. *What on earth has Celia Rees's "Calling the Cats" to do with all these others?* I asked myself. Then, re-reading, thinking about it, I could see that the link had to do with the young protagonist, in this case a girl named Julia—called Jules—coming from a difficult, disconnected past, finding a way to lay her problems to rest at last. I read the story one final time and could see the grief in it, the loneliness, the well-intentioned mom and the girl with the secret knowledge, the solitary thing she had to do, in order to find her own *somewhere*.

Not different at all. Just one author's new way of looking at the same hard issues.

Happy endings? Some. Maybe. But youth is not a time when there are *any* endings, really. Just coming-to-terms-with. "Resigned" is a title with more than one meaning. Mom quits, in this story by Meg Rosoff. She resigns from the family. And does she rejoin it after they have all thought things over? No. *"So this is where I'm supposed to say we all lived happily ever after, but in fact we didn't—at least, not quite in the way we expected to,"* the young narrator says as the story approaches its conclusion.

This family comes to terms with how things are. They become resigned, and somehow content as well.

And maybe that is what today's young people are best at and may find in this collection: a new way of seeing things, a new way of being, of finding their place, a peek into the *"somewhere* I can be just me." With that understanding, they can move forward; trudging, sometimes; battling, certainly; but radiant, always, with the wonderful resilience that the young seem always to have. *Shining on.*

—Lois Lowry

Meg Rosoff

RESIGNED

My mother has resigned.

Not from her job, but from being a mother. She said she'd had enough, more than enough. In actual fact, she used what my dad calls certain good old-fashioned Anglo-Saxon words that they're allowed to use and we're not. She said we could bring ourselves up from now on, she wanted no more part in it.

She said what she did all day was the laundry, the cooking, the shopping, the cleaning, the making the beds, the clearing the table, the packing and unpacking the dishwasher, the dragging everyone to ballet and piano and cello and football and swimming, not to mention school, the shouting at everyone to get ready, the making sure everyone had the right kit for the right event, the making cakes for school cake sales, the helping with homework, the making the garden look nice, the feeding the fish we couldn't be bothered to feed, the walking the dog we'd begged to have and then ignored, the making packed lunches for school according to what we would and wouldn't eat (for those of us who have packed lunches) and then the unmaking them after school with all the things we didn't eat, the remembering dinner money (for those of us who didn't want packed lunches), and not to mention, she said, all the nagging in between.

Here she paused, which was good because we all thought the strain of talking so fast without stopping was going to make her pass out. But quick as a flash she was off again. Dad stood grinning in the corner, by the way, like all this had nothing at all to do with him, but we knew it was just a matter of time before she remembered she was married and then the you-know-what was going to hit the you-know-who.

Mum took a deep breath.

And another thing.

She had her fingers out for this one. And there weren't enough fingers in the room to list the next set of crimes.

Who did we think took care of the bank accounts, the car insurance, the life insurance, the mortgage, the tax returns, the milk bill, the charity donations, the accountant . . .

Here she paused again, looking around the kitchen to make absolutely certain she had our full attention and eye contact and no one was thinking of escape—even for a minute or two—from the full force of her resentment.

We are not totally stupid, by the way. We read the tabloids often enough to know that between a mother giving a lecture of the fanatical nervous breakdown variety to her kids and Grievous Bodily Harm there is a very fine line indeed. The *Sun*, for instance, seems to specialize in stories along the lines of *Formerly average mum bludgeons family with stern lecture and tire iron, then makes cup of tea*. We three kids were doing the eye contact and respectful hangdog-look thing, maintaining that pathetic silence that makes mothers feel guilty eventually, when they're done shouting. But we had to give the old girl credit, this time she showed no sign of flagging.

She took another deep breath.

. . . the magazine subscriptions, the dentist appointments, the birthday parties, the Christmas dinner, the presents, the nephews and nieces, the *in-laws*.

As one, we swiveled to look at Dad. Mum had stopped and was looking at Dad too, whose brain you could tell was racing with possible escape routes, excuses, mitigating circumstances, and of course the desire to be somewhere else entirely. He shot a single furtive glance at the back door, figured it was too far to risk making a break for it. (Mum is no slouch in the lunge-and-tackle stakes, having been a county champion lacrosse player on a team full of hairy dykes back a hundred years ago when she was in school. We knew she hadn't forgotten all the moves due to an incident a few years ago with an attempted purse-snatching. None of us refers to it now, but word on the street is that the guy still never leaves the house.)

And, she said (glaring at me because the woman is an experienced enough mother to hear you thinking a digression about lacrosse), *and* I hope you are listening, because when I say I am not going to do it anymore, I mean *I am not going to do it anymore*. She glared at each one of us in turn— a kind of equal-opportunity glare.

And one last thing, she said, in an even scarier, quieter voice, and I risked a sideways glance to see if Francis Ford Coppola was in the wings directing this masterful performance. *From this moment on*, she continued, I am deaf to whining. Deaf to any annoying tone of voice *you three*— she shot a relatively benign look at Dad just to let him know he was off the hook on this particular issue, assuming he backed her up, that is—*can dream up*. Screaming will only be acknowledged if accompanied by bones sticking out of skin or hatchet actually *buried* in skull.

Moe was shuffling his feet a little now, and sneaking peeks at his watch because his teacher hated it when anyone was late to school.

She glared at him and he jumped to attention like someone out of the Queen's Guard.

Right, she said, surveying her troops and appearing a little calmer now. Any questions?

Nobody dared say anything, except, of course, Alec, who could smarm for England and has not lived fifteen years on this earth without picking up a trick or two along the way. He had stopped lounging against the wall, which is what he does with most of his waking hours, stood up fairly straight, plastered this sickening look of sincerity across his wily mug and said, OK, Mum, fair cop, we're with you on this. I'm only surprised you didn't make a stand a long time ago.

Then, just to prove she wasn't born yesterday either, Mum made this kind of snorting sound and rolled her eyes, indicating rejection of smarm, and said, I can't tell you how pleased I am that you approve, Alec. Now everyone better get a move on because school starts in twenty minutes and *you* are going to have to figure out how to get there.

As one, we turned to Dad, who was now trying to make himself two-dimensional and slide behind the fridge, which would have been easier if he hadn't been six-foot-four and built like a rugby scrum half. But Dad is a man who knows when to fold in poker, like when all he's got in his hand are twos, threes, and fours of different colors. He folded gracefully.

Come on then, he said in a resigned voice. Pile in. We'll leave Mum alone for now and give her some time to collect herself.

Some time to collect myself? Mum said. *Some* time *to collect myself?* How kind, how fantastically kind of you. Why, I can't think *how* to show my appreciation short of taking out a full-page ad in the *effing Financial Times*. (She practically screamed that last bit.) But, say what you will. I now have *the rest of my life* to myself, and it's you suckers who are going to have to cope.

She smiled at us then, a genuine smile, all warm and mumsy and loving, and kissed us each in turn, the way you'd kiss people who were trooping off to a firing squad.

Have a lovely day, all of you. See you later.

We hated it when she turned all nice and snatched the moral high ground out from under us. But it was getting late so we all crammed into Dad's car, elbowing and kicking and biting each other like captives in a government crocodile-breeding initiative, and headed off to be late to school.

Naturally there was a fair bit of conversation in the car about Mum's little episode.

She's bluffing, Alec said. She's probably just getting her period.

I wouldn't be so sure, smart-arse, Dad said. She didn't look like she was bluffing to me. And just a tip for later life—don't ever even *think* those words in the vicinity of a woman or you'll find yourself castrated before you can say oops.

Moe grinned and I sniggered, knowing our dear big brother's future was definitely going to be bollock-free.

Anyway, we got to school late, and all of us got detention, except Moe, who has a professional way of looking like he's about to burst into tears. By lunchtime we'd all forgotten that we even had a mum at home, what with all the gossip and sexual harassment and who's not talking to who and have you noticed who *she*'s hanging around with these days to talk about.

After school, Moe and I caught a ride home with Esther's mum, who wears flowery clothes and acts like a proper mum, asking if you're hungry and doling out crisps and having tissues with her at all times, and never screaming *shut the bloody **** up!* at her children like someone else I can think of. Not that I'd want her as my mum, due to her being an irony-free zone, not to mention harboring a fervent wish for Esther to grow up to be a Person of Substance, an expression she actually uses in public, which explains why Esther looks so long-suffering and wants to be a flight attendant.

My mum always said she wanted me to be a ballerina, which is her idea of the world's funniest joke because I'm not exactly small and could be two ballerinas if they cut me in half and I had four legs. Moe wants to be a vet, like every other eight-year-old, and Alec just wants to get out of school, drink alcohol, go clubbing, get his driver's license, get a car, and have a girlfriend who'll let him have sex with her all the time, though not necessarily in that order.

But I'm getting off the point here.

We stayed at Esther's for supper, dutifully notifying Mum so she couldn't shout that she'd gone to all the trouble to make us a nice blah blah blah with three kinds of blah blah blah on the side and we weren't there to eat it and hadn't even had the courtesy to phone.

She seemed pleased to hear that we weren't coming

home for dinner, and it wasn't until I hung up that I realized she hadn't said the usual—if you're not home by seven, you're toast—but I took it as tacit and made sure Esther's mum gave us a ride home. We walked in the door at ten to seven, which I thought was a pretty good touch, just in case someone's watch might be running a few minutes fast.

Mum was on the phone when we got there, talking to her business partner, Jo. They'd had a lot of interest from America after the article that was written about them in *Country Life*, and apparently antique garden implements were all the rage among rich Americans who had too much money and not enough antique garden implements.

I noticed immediately that the breakfast table looked exactly the same as it had when we all left for school that morning, with dirty dishes and open jars of marmalade and crumbs everywhere, and I thought Mum was going a bit far to prove a point, given how much she hates mess of any kind, but I thought I'd better play along and so started clearing up. I shouted for Alec to come help, but he said he didn't give a monkey's whether it was cleared up or not, and since we were in charge we should be able to live in squalor if squalor was what we liked.

As squalor went, this was pretty tame, and anyway I had homework to do and got distracted by Hooligan wanting to go out for a walk and since Mum wasn't giving orders anymore, I let him out in the garden and even he looked confused that no one was shouting at him to stay away from the herbaceous borders.

Hey, Moe, I hissed. Get this. And I pointed to Hoo out in the garden doing a poo the size of Mont-Saint-Michel by Mum's *Nicotiana sylvestris*, and Moe's eyes widened and we both thought, cool!

After that we forgot about Hoo and watched some television while pretending to do homework and in the commercial breaks I managed to write a whole essay entitled "The Egyptians: Why They Became Extinct."

After the initial shock, this new regime was turning out to be much more relaxing than life with Mussolini. Oops, did I say a fanatic Italian dictator? I meant Mum.

When Dad finally got home he looked a little grumpy about no dinner being on the table, but it wasn't long till he got the hang of things and filled a soup bowl full of Frosties and sighed really loud a few times to make sure everyone knew he wasn't thrilled about the new order. Moe looked at Dad's Frosties and, because no one said no, he had some too.

Over the next week or so, Mum moved into her office in the garden, which she'd had the foresight to make Dad build with its own shower room and enough of a kitchen to survive on. Also, as she put it, there was no way she was going to step foot in the kitchen until we four called pest control. She still came to say good night to us, a little like a fond auntie, and sometimes we hung around and did our homework in her office because every place in the whole house seemed to have something messing up the surfaces where you might want to put a book. And she didn't seem to mind us coming in as long as we didn't bother her or leave wrappers on the floor. Which was tricky, given that all our meals seemed to come in wrappers these days. She was on the phone a lot, and having meetings with her partner and smiling more than we'd seen in ages.

Which was great.

Only, after a few weeks of this, us kids were starting to look at each other and think, hey, fun's fun, but there are no clean clothes in the whole house and we've run out of cereal for breakfast and tea, and speaking of tea, there's only one manky box of teabags that came free from Tesco about a hundred years ago and Dad's taken to drinking instant coffee, which puts him in an even worse mood than he is naturally. Also, the dog needs brushing, the radiators make a horrible noise, and every envelope that arrives has *For Your Urgent Attention* written on it in red.

So we sat down that Saturday at what had once been the breakfast table but now looked like that exhibit at the zoo, filled with half-eaten meals and *Rattus norvegicus* probably written on a brass plaque somewhere. I noticed the two goldfish in the bowl on top of the fridge for the first time in ages, and it was clear no one else had noticed them either, considering that they had given up swimming some time ago and taken up floating on the surface. Moe was wearing the cleanest of his shirts, which had ketchup spilled down the front and a chip actually stuck to it, Dad had gone out to have breakfast alone with the newspaper at Starbucks, and Alec and I were drinking blueberry cordial, which was the only thing left to drink in the house since we ran out of teabags and the milkman stopped coming.

OK, guys, I said. I think it's time to start begging.

Moe looked annoyed. But we're doing perfectly well without any help, he said, digging into a bowl of recently thawed peas from the freezer with some week-old takeaway curry mixed in.

Alec said he was going to be sick and Moe should be taken into care, and they began to shout at each other and Alec stormed out, but I called him back because it was so obvious to all of us that something had to be done. We managed to be civil to each other long enough to write a letter setting out our terms of surrender. Here's what we wrote:

> Dearest Mum,
>
> You were right. Even we can't live with ourselves.
>
> If you agree to come back we will follow any rules you make with absolutely no complaining and no whining.
>
> Promise. Cross our hearts and hope to die.
>
> Please. We miss you so much.
>
> Plus, we were wrong.
>
> Love,
> Your children

I typed the letter up on Dad's laptop, set it in a nice curly font, and after I printed it out we all signed it and drew hearts on it and so forth to suck up, and then we slipped it under the door of the studio and went back into the house and got to work.

It took all day, so it wasn't a bad thing that we didn't hear back from her right away. We scrubbed the floors and the walls, the kitchen and the bathroom, we swept off all the junk piled on every surface and separated out the bills and left them neatly stacked, and Dad paid them when he got home. Moe cleaned out the refrigerator and Alec and I went up to the shop with a lifetime's supply of pocket money and bought food—not the stuff we'd been eating all month, like chocolate breakfast bars, but proper food, like chicken parts and green beans and granary bread and cheddar cheese. We cleaned out the fishbowl and flushed both the fish down the toilet, which wasn't inhumane considering their advanced state of fatality, put clean sheets on all the beds and did about fifteen loads of laundry, and even folded it up afterwards. Alec got out the Hoover, but miracles have to end somewhere, and when the phone rang and it was his girlfriend, I ended up doing it myself.

It was a not entirely unsatisfying day, if I say so myself. Even the house itself seemed less bad-tempered, like it preferred being clean.

Well, Mum may have suspected something was up when she saw all the black rubbish bags stacked outside by the front door, or she might just have got tired of sleeping on the little daybed in the studio. Or maybe she even missed us. Who knows.

But that night, around ten p.m., we saw lights on in the studio, and later found a handwritten note pushed through the letter box.

It read, *I'll think about it. Love, Mum.*

And I guess she thought about it all day Sunday, because it was teatime on Sunday when she finally knocked on the door like a visitor, and when we let her in, she looked around in every room, and nodded every now and then, and finally she sat down at the (immaculate) kitchen table and said, OK, I'll come back.

We all started cheering and surrounded her and hugged and kissed her, but she held up one hand and continued.

On one condition. At which point she pulled out a sheaf of papers that looked a little like the Treaty of Versailles, and handed one set to each of us, and on it was a schedule of who did what job on what day and, to be fair, she had written herself into the list occasionally too.

So this is where I'm supposed to say we all lived happily ever after, but in fact we didn't—at least, not quite in the way we expected to. Nobody really stuck to the jobs listed on the piece of paper, including Mum, because she was away a lot suddenly due to her business being so successful at last, but the good thing was she seemed to care a lot less about the house being as clean as it was before, and we learned one important lesson—not to push her past a certain point—so we did pitch in more than we ever had, with the possible exception of Alec. Then Mum really started raking in the dough and Dad quit his job and stayed home, doing most of the cooking and cleaning and gardening and seeming strangely happy about it. So in general, things worked out more or less peacefully for a while.

But a few months later, we noticed Mum was spending a lot of time talking to the young guy next door, and one day she gathered us together and said she was moving out for good. We just stood there stunned and completely freaked out, and Moe began to cry, and Mum grabbed him up in her arms and said stop crying, Moe, and come look at my new house.

Then she opened the front door, and jumped over the little wall by the front path and pulled a key out of her pocket and opened the door of the house next door. And while we were staring at her trying to figure out what had happened, she was grinning ear to ear and said I've finally sorted it.

So that's the end of the story. Mum bought the house next door from the young guy, and though we have to take our shoes off when we go visit her, she almost never shouts at us anymore, and she never complains about the mess in our house, not ever. And when I get fed up living with Dad or if I can't stand another minute with Moe and Alec, I move in with Mum for a few weeks and we have a great time staying up late and talking and just getting on. And sometimes we rent a movie and make popcorn and invite Mum round to our house to watch it and she stays over, and we make her breakfast in the morning before she goes back to work.

And whenever anyone asks us in a polite concerned voice why we don't live with our mother, we put on mournful faces and sigh and say, Well, she just walked out on us one day, but we're pretty much resigned to it now.

And then we fall about laughing, and go and tell Mum.

Meg Cabot

ALLIE FINKLESTEIN's RULES FOR BOYFRIENDS

From: SoccerStud@andrewshigh.edu
To: CheerGrrl@andrewshigh.edu
Saturday, November 3, 3:00 p.m.

I know you've been seeing that freak Greg
Harding behind my back. Don't try to deny
it. Steve Dewitter's little brother Jeff
said he spied you and Greg through the living room window while he was mowing the
lawn, and that Greg had his tongue down your
throat (while he was supposed to be "tutoring" you in geometry). Truthfully, Allie, I
really never thought it would end this way.
But maybe it's all for the best. Anyone who

```
would go out with a geek like Greg deserves
what she gets.
```

```
Been nice knowing you. Oh, and say hi to Greg
for me.
```

Allie Finklestein's Diary
PRIVATE! KEEP OUT!
THIS MEANS YOU, MOM!!!!
Saturday, November 3, 3:30 p.m.

OK, there is something seriously wrong with this picture. I go to the mall to see if I can find a non-see-through black bra to go under my see-through black Betsey Johnson blouse, which I was planning on wearing to Kimmy Davis's party tonight, and I come home, and what do I find in my in-box?

Yeah. That'd be an e-mail from my boyfriend, breaking up with me.

I guess I'm still in shock, because I don't feel anything yet.

Except maybe a little heartburn from the Cinnabon I ate for lunch.

Wait . . . maybe it isn't heartburn. *Maybe this is what it feels like to get dumped.* I'll have to remember to ask Stephanie.

But you know, Stephanie totally cried when Todd dumped her outside the Loews Cineplex right before last year's spring formal. And I don't feel like crying.

Then again, I didn't run out and buy a six-hundred-dollar Nicole Miller evening gown and rip the tags off as soon as I got it home so I couldn't return it if my no-good bohunk of a boyfriend dumped me the night before the dance. Like Steph did.

Maybe that's why she was crying so much. Because of the Visa bill she knew her mom was going to get.

There must be something wrong with me. You know, on account of the whole not crying thing.

But in a way, it's kind of . . . well, a relief. I mean, Cal NEVER followed my rules. He was completely unsupportive of the fact that I want the night I lose my virginity to be *special*, not some grope-fest in his sweaty-sock-smelling bedroom while his parents are seeing *Man of La Mancha* or something at the Chevy Chase Dinner Theater. There should be clean sheets involved, at the very least. And my name spelled in rose petals on the pillows. And a new episode of *America's Next Top Model* to watch afterwards.

All that, on top of the fact that he was always asking me to *Touch It*. Like I was going to go anywhere *near* It. Especially in his *car*.

The truth is, I'm relieved to be rid of him.

And that thing with Greg Harding? Hello, perfectly innocent. He was talking about obtuse angles and I couldn't get over how cute his lips looked every time he said the word *obtuse*. I just *had* to start kissing them.

And it was really . . . nice. Especially since he never once asked me to Touch It.

And Greg is a surprisingly good kisser, for a guy I'm pretty sure has never been out with a girl before. It must be from all the practice he's had on that trombone he plays in band.

But there were no tongues involved. Please! I don't know what Steve Dewitter's little brother thinks he saw, but Cal knows perfectly well I'm not that kind of girl. At least, not with a guy who's never even taken me out for sashimi.

Cal probably thinks I'm going to call or text him as soon as I get his e-mail, begging him to take me back.

Boy, is he in for a surprise. Goodbye, Cal. Nice knowing you. Glad I didn't waste my hymen on YOU. Not that I have a hymen anymore, because I'm pretty sure it got broken at horse camp that summer I turned ten.

Oh, Pancho! What a better boyfriend you'd have made than Cal! YOU knew how to follow the rules. I only had to pull on your reins to get you to stop. I should have stuck with you.

Breakfast:
One glass OJ
Diet Coke
Low-fat yogurt, raspberry

Lunch:
Cinnabon
7 (!!!!!) Do-Si-Do peanut butter Girl Scout
    cookies

19

Pack of Twizzlers
Calorie Total: 2,415 (!!!!!)

Note to self: Tell Jilly not to leave open Girl Scout cookie boxes lying around!!!!

From: PartyPrincess@andrewshigh.edu
To: CheerGrrl@andrewshigh.edu
Saturday, November 3, 4:10 p.m.

OMG, Allie, do u have any idea what Cal is going around saying about u? He's saying Steve's little brother Jeff saw u making out with GREG HARDING. GREG HARDING, that weird guy who plays Dungeons and Dragons and the TROMBONE in band and talks about The Matrix all the time.

U better get back together with Cal, or ur social cred could be totally ruined by Christmas, and then the squad might vote on a new cheer captain next semester. I'm just saying.

C u at Kimmy's party.

Allie Finklestein's Diary
PRIVATE! KEEP OUT!
THIS MEANS YOU, MOM!!!!
Saturday, November 3, 5:00 p.m.

Whatever. So I got a D on my last geometry quiz (I guess I should have paid less attention to the way Greg's lips looked and more to what they were actually saying). I still don't see what the big deal is. It's not like I'm not going to get into a good college just because I've got a D in ONE CLASS. I have excellent recommendations and tons of extracurriculars. There isn't a college in America that wouldn't be lucky to have me. Especially after the way I got the PTA to cave on the halter-top issue. I totally agree that there are certain people who should NEVER be allowed to wear halter tops—like that girl in my French class (with the back fat), for instance—but every other cheerleading squad in the county wears halters! We looked like total dorks out there in our stupid Andrews High *sweaters*. It was EMBARRASSING.

I don't know what Mom and Dad are so worried about. Like you even need to know geometry to succeed in the world of fashion design. I mean, did Donatella Versace's parents give HER a hard time about her geometry scores? If they even *have* geometry in Italy, which I highly doubt?

I rest my case.

Surprisingly, Mom and Dad were less than receptive to this argument. They even had the nerve to suggest I stay home from Kimmy's party tonight, and have an emergency tutoring session with Greg instead. Which is clearly an example of nerd prejudice, since they seemed to just assume he'd be available.

Stay home and study. On a SATURDAY night!

After I was through laughing I saw they were totally serious. So I had no choice but to tell them about Cal's e-mail (I couldn't *show* it to them, of course, because then they'd know I've been making out with my geometry tutor, which I will admit doesn't cast me in the best light, and could even lead to poor Greg getting fired—though the tongue-down-the-throat accusation in Cal's e-mail is totally libelous). And so, of course, I *have* to go to the party—I need to put my heartbreak behind me.

It was quite a performance, if I do say so myself. I even managed to summon up a few tears. Well, OK, not tears, *exactly*. But I was so scared about having to stay home that my throat got very dry and so my voice cracked a few times as I was telling them about my new, single-woman status.

They were even happier than I'd thought they'd be. Oh, they ACTED like they were sad for me, but a little while ago I overheard them toasting one another with glasses of Diet Pepsi and going, "Buh-bye, Cal," and laughing like hyenas.

I know they didn't like him—and they didn't even KNOW about the Touch It thing—but that is just plain childish.

Anyway, the upshot is, I get to go out tonight after all.

Because I need my friends around to support me during this time of grief, and all. Although Mom assured me that if I wanted, she and I could stay home together and watch *Pretty Woman* and eat macadamia brittle ice cream right out of the carton (um, hello, since when do hookers and ice cream make everything OK?). She wanted me to know that it was all right to mourn (!!!!) my loss.

When I said no way was I going to waste my first opportunity to wear my new Capucine-Puerari bra, she cupped my face and told me she's always admired my fierce courage.

Good thing neither of them has seen the Betsey Johnson blouse. Then they'd really learn a thing or two about courage.

I wish everybody would quit bothering me about all this. I have on a St. Ives mud mask, and my constantly having to reassure people that I'm all right is making it crack.

Note to self: Next time mud mask is applied, make sure no one else is home.

Dinner:
Diet Pepsi
Leftover lasagna
Salad with no-fat ranch dressing
9 Do-Si-Dos
Calorie Total: 1,925

WHY MUST JILLY LEAVE HER GIRL SCOUT COOK-IES LYING AROUND THE HOUSE?????

From: CheerGrrl@andrewshigh.edu
To: PartyPrincess@andrewshigh.edu
Saturday, November 3, 6:00 p.m.

Have you been sniffing your Sephora eyelash
glue again? I am not getting back together
with Cal.

And Greg isn't obsessed with The Matrix, he's
obsessed with the idea that consumer society
forms a kind of code that gives individuals
the illusion of choice while in fact entrap-
ping them in a vast web of simulated reality.

God. Get a clue, Tiffany.

See you at Kimmy's.

Allie Finklestein's Diary
PRIVATE! KEEP OUT!
THIS MEANS YOU, MOM!!!!
Saturday, November 3, 11:00 p.m.

Could my friends BE more annoying? I thought my *family*
was bad, but tonight was ridiculous. I walk through the
door to Kimmy's party, and next thing I know, half the female population of Andrews High is dragging me into the

kitchen, telling me they heard about Cal dumping me, and asking if I'm all right.

Just because I'm not bawling my eyes out like Steph did when she got dumped, or stuffing my face like Kimmy when she found out about Chad and that girl from the video arcade (*note to self: TELL NO ONE ABOUT THE DO-SI-DOS*), they all think I'm some kind of martyr. You know, weeping on the inside, and all of that. Even Tiffany was all, "It's OK, Allie. You're around friends. You can cry if you want to. We don't mind."

Yeah, that's just what you'd like me to do, wouldn't you, Tiffany? Cry until my mascara runs (ha, as if: I totally have waterproof on) so you can tell the squad I'm too "emotionally unstable" at the moment to make any decisions about the choreography for State. So not going to happen, Tiffany. Number one, because I will never cry over a mere GUY, and number two, because I'd sooner die than give you the satisfaction, you shallow cow.

Then Tiffany had to start in about how maybe the reason I wasn't crying was because what Steve Dewitter's little brother was going around saying was true—the thing about me and Greg, I mean—and that maybe the reason I wasn't more upset about Cal was because *I was in love with Greg Harding.*

Instead of the truth, which is that I'm not more upset because I got freaking tired of being asked to *Touch It* all the time.

Fortunately Tiff's statement got quite a laugh from all the other girls on the squad.

Except that I could tell Tiffany was totally serious.

What is her GLITCH, anyway?

The worst part was, *I didn't say anything*. I didn't say, "Um, excuse me, Tiffany, but Steve Dewitter's little brother is right." I didn't say, "You know what, Tiffany? Yeah, I did make out with Greg Harding. And it was *great*. And if the squad—or you—has a problem with that, you can all kiss the back pocket of my True Religions."

I don't know WHY I didn't say anything like that. Especially when Tiffany started in about how, in my e-mail to her, I'd almost sounded like I LIKED Greg Harding. She said she'd almost expected me to start spouting off about how we need to end nerd persecution in our lifetime, or something.

It was right about then that I decided I'd had enough party fun and started looking for a ride home (obviously, I had to find my own way, since Tiffany said she wasn't ready to leave yet).

I had a choice between Dan Friedman ("Yeah, sure I'll give you a lift. Hey, my parents are out of town—have you ever gotten high on a water bed?"), Bill Stoddard ("What? No, I'm totally OK to drive. I've only had, what, like six beers.") and Chad Harlowe ("I've got a plasma screen in the backseat." *Wink. Wink.*).

So I decided to call Greg on the off chance he was home. Not because I LIKE him. Well, not like that. But he lives right around the corner from Kimmy, and I know it would be totally easy for him to come and pick me up.

And it turns out he WAS home, hosting a Dungeons and Dragons party, or whatever they call them. Meetings? Seminars?

Anyway, he said it was OK for him to take a break because he was the Dungeon Master, whatever that is, and everybody had to obey his commands. He told me he'd be right over.

But I told him I'd come over to HIS house and meet him there instead.

I swear it wasn't because I didn't want Tiffany and those guys to see me getting into his car, or anything. I really just wanted a breath of fresh air, to sort of clear my head.

Then when I got there and found him waiting for me in his driveway, I don't know what came over me, but before we even had our seat belts on, I was like, "Greg, thanks so much for driving me home. You must really think I'm *obtuse*," and he was like, "Why, Allie, I don't think you're *obtuse* at all."

And then of course I couldn't help myself, I had to kiss him again. This time with tongue.

So I guess the truth is, I DO like him.

That Way.

A lot.

So then while he was recovering from my tongue being in his mouth, which sort of seemed to send him into a coma, I decided to give him The Speech . . . you know, about how any guy who wants to be Allie Finklestein's Boyfriend has to:

1) Ask me on proper dates, which means meals only at restaurants with actual metal silverware (unless it's sashimi, in which case, chopsticks, but real ones, not those kind you pull apart and get all splintery), not fast food.

2) Come to my house to meet my parents (which he's already done, because, duh, they pay him twenty bucks an hour to tutor me).

3) Finance all movie tickets. I will pay for refreshments.

4) Not ask me to Touch It, and no Doing It till Prom. And then only if he's confessed his undying love for me and sworn he'd never even think of looking at another girl, especially Tiffany Haynes.

To which Greg replied he'd never in a million years look at Tiffany Haynes, whom he finds obtuse . . . which I'm pretty sure he didn't say just to get me to kiss him again. Even though I did. I mean, he can't KNOW what that word does to me . . . can he?

And then after we'd kissed for a while, he was like, "Touch what?"

Oh, God. I can't believe this. *Greg Harding might be the perfect guy for me.*

Note to self: Febreze Betsey Johnson blouse. Something at Kimmy's party was RANK and got into clothes. Possibly Bill Stoddard. Smell, not Bill. Got into clothes, I mean. Duh.

Party food:
Two Diet Cokes
Handful Chex Party Mix
Five peanuts
One jalapeño popper
5 Listerine strips (to cover jalapeño popper breath. Good thing I had them with me, too, considering what went on in Greg's car!)
Calorie total: 325

From: PartyPrincess@andrewshigh.edu
To: CheerGrrl@andrewshigh.edu
Sunday, November 4, 4:25 p.m.

U are so busted. Stephanie's cousin's best friend's boyfriend Bud was playing Dungeons and Dragons over at Greg Harding's last night, when Greg suddenly told them he had to leave to take u home, and not to roll while he was gone.

If u want to resign your position as cheer captain now, it will spare us having to vote u out on Monday.

From: CheerGrrl@andrewshigh.edu
To: PartyPrincess@andrewshigh.edu
Sunday, November 4, 4:31 p.m.

Um, this may come as a surprise to you, Tiff, but I am NOT resigning my position as cheer captain. Because unlike you, Tiffany, I do not plan to spend the rest of my life doing basket tosses, gliding along in my Capucine-Puerari bra and see-through Betsey Johnson blouses, never feeling anything, never loving—or being loved—by any man. Unlike you, Tiffany, I can't be satisfied to spend my free time with a CALORIE COUNTER and MY USCA CHAMPIONSHIP PIN. OK? I need REAL CONVERSATION and COMPANIONSHIP, which Greg Harding provides me. I LOVE GREG. AND HE LOVES ME.

And you know what? Even if I DO get voted off the team, I have WAY more important things to worry about right now than that, such as becoming a well-rounded, interesting individual, capable of contributing in myriad ways to society, and also cutting down on my saturated fat intake. Oh, and passing geometry and all.

So, in closing, you, Tiffany, could not BE more obtuse.

From: PartyPrincess@andrewshigh.edu
To: CheerGrrl@andrewshigh.edu
Sunday, November 4, 4:43 p.m.

God, have a coronary, why don't u? I was totally kidding. I don't care who u go out with. Especially since—I might as well tell u now—last night after u left Kimmy's, I fully made out with Cal. I hope that's OK. But u kept telling us all you were over him.

There's just one thing though . . . he kept asking me to touch it. What was he talking about?

Anyway, congrats to u and Nerd Boy. U know, I heard trombone players really know how to kiss.

PS: What does obtuse mean??????

Melvin Burgess

COMING HOME

I'd come home early from school. It was a hot day. I let myself in and went to the kitchen to get some juice out of the fridge. As I stood there swigging orange out of the carton, I looked out the kitchen window. There, tucked down behind the shed, was my mum having a snog with some bloke. They were dappled with shadow from the trees. Her blouse was unbuttoned, hanging open. They were kissing each other very hard, and he kept crushing her up into his chest and sliding his hands under her blouse at the back.

I ducked out of sight. I felt a bit like James Bond, hiding there with my back to the wall, the carton of juice in my hand like a gun. Then I peeped round again to have another look. I wanted to see if he was going to take her clothes off.

They were smiling now. She put her hands round his face and kissed him in a way I never saw her kiss my dad. It was like a film. It was so unreal, it made me think of fairies at the bottom of the garden. I felt that if I took a picture of it, it wouldn't come out. He pushed her up against the shed wall and slid his hands down to her bum. I could see her hands stroking the back of his neck.

I walked back to the front door, opened it, slammed it hard, and then wandered about shouting, "I'm home, Mum, I'm home! Mum, I'm home!" at the top of my voice. I went back into the kitchen and pretended to get the juice out of the fridge again and didn't look out that window.

"Mum, I'm home!" I bellowed. I went into the sitting room and turned on the TV. There was nothing on. It was only half past two. We'd been let out of school early. Mum should have been at work. There was a school program about geology and I watched that.

They came into the house a couple of minutes later. I could hear their voices.

". . . yes, nice to see you."

"And you. We'll get that trip organized, then."

"OK."

"Right . . ."

"Cup of tea?"

"No, better go . . ."

They walked down the hall and stopped outside the door. Mum's head popped in.

"You're home early, Laurence," she said.

"So are you."

"They let us off early."

"Same here."

Outside the door a voice called, "Hi, Laurence."

"Oh, hi, Nigel."

Nigel Turner. Mr. Turner. Someone from her school. There was a pause and then he said, "I better be off, Sandra." She walked him to the door. I ran to the window to see him. I caught him standing right next to his car, and he looked over his shoulder full into my face, but I didn't run away or even flinch. We stared at each other for a second; then he opened the car door and got in, and I went back to the TV.

Mum came back and said, "Hello, darling, good day?"

"Sure."

She said, "How did you know I was home, Laurence?"

"Dunno," I said.

I could feel her staring at me. "Must've seen your bag or something."

"You're home early," she said again.

For the first time I looked up at her. She tried to smile. I smiled back, but my face must have looked like a cartoon. I looked back at the telly and waited while she left the room.

I thought, she knows I know, and I know she knows I know. I expected her to have a little talk with me, which is what usually happens in our house if there're any problems, but she never said a thing about it. She was scared. . . . You see? Chicken.

My sister, Gill, came home later and we sat and watched TV and ate crisps together, but I never said anything to her about it. She's sixteen, two years older than me, and she's always giving me advice about girls.

Once I said to her, "What do you know about girls?"

And she said, "I *am* a girl."

"Not a proper one," I said.

She got up in a huff. "Can't you take anything seriously?" she snapped.

"Only if it's worth it," I said, and she rolled her eyes and stamped out. But I was being serious, she *doesn't* know anything about girls, not the kind of girls I want to go out with. The kind of girls I want to go out with would *like* me talking like that.

I once caught my mum and dad having sex, you know. I went into the room without knocking and she was sitting on top of him. I hadn't thought at the time, but looking back I could hear her making pleased-sounding noises before I went in. I didn't really know what it was at the time, but Gill told me. She said it must have been. It didn't look anything like what Mum was doing with this other bloke, though.

The day after I saw her and Nigel Turner, I remember standing by my bedroom window, which is above the kitchen, looking down into the garden where they'd been and saying to myself, "She has a lover," but I still couldn't make it as though it had really happened. I said, "Sandra," to myself. We always called her Mum. Even though that woman down there with her blouse open had been my mum, it wasn't the same person who cooked and worked and shopped and woke up every morning smelling of Dad.

When I was younger, a few years ago, I used to try to see my mum with nothing on. I used to peep through the key-hole of the bedroom. . . . Well, I'd never seen a real woman in the nude. I hadn't done it for years, but now I wanted to see her like that again. I was handing the dishes to her after dinner a few days later. I was fed up thinking about it when-ever I saw her. She still hadn't said anything to me. She was bending over, putting the plates in the dishwasher, and I was looking at her back. I was wondering what was it that made Nigel Turner so turned on. She had on this slightly transparent blouse—you could see her bra strap under it, and where the flesh squeezed out on either side. I reached down, I took the strap in my fingers and I snapped it.

She looked up at me as if I'd hit her. "What did you do that for, Laurence?" she exclaimed.

I shrugged. "I dunno." Well, I didn't know . . . I just did it.

She scowled; she was really furious. She stood up and yelled in my face, "You're not to do that to me again. Do you understand?"

"Yeah, sure, so what?"

Then she stamped off out of the room. I was really angry. It was just a joke. It didn't mean anything, it was a joke. Maybe I did it harder than I'd meant to. I thought she should be grateful to me, really. I could have said something if I'd wanted. I thought, what would happen if I told my dad?

It was at dinner. Dad always says, "The family that eats together stays together." He's done nearly all the cooking ever since he went part-time at the school where he teaches. He used to be Head of English, but it was too much work for him. Now he thinks how lucky we all are because we can have home-cooked food three or four times during the week and not just at weekends. Sometimes he even bakes bread. The bread's nice, and sometimes he does nice meals, but I prefer meals out of a packet.

Someone said my name.

"What?"

"Pass the sauce, deafo," said Gill.

"Sorry."

I had this plan about making loads of money by blackmailing my mum. I could threaten to tell my dad unless she gave me loads of money. I could make her write her will out in my favor. I could make her give me tenners whenever I wanted. Then Gill would always be saying, "Where did you get all that?" and I'd just go, "Ah ha! Nothing for noses," like she does to me whenever I ask her anything.

"Laurence!"

"What?"

"Not what—pardon."

"What?"

"Christ. Do you want more fish pie?"

"No, thanks."

"You're in a dream."

I *was* in a dream. I could make a fortune. Out of Nigel Turner, too. He was married. I think he and his wife had even come to dinner sometime. I could blackmail both of them. I'd be the richest kid in the school. I could have anything I liked. It would be great.

Mum and Dad started bickering. Dad wanted Mum to go part-time, like him. He was saying it was too much stress working full-time at a school these days. He was saying how bad-tempered and distant she was. He was always going on about all these other teachers who were having nervous breakdowns and falling to bits, and that she should get out and go part-time before it happened to her and he was left having to pay all the bills on half a wage and run the house all on his own.

"We could have days out. We could walk or visit places. Look . . . I can do anything I want on Mondays, Tuesdays and Friday afternoons. You could do it with me," he said.

"But I *like* working full-time," she said.

"Well, I think it's selfish of you," said my dad. "Life's to enjoy, not to work yourself into the ground."

"I'm not working myself into the ground."

"Then why are you so distant? If you're married with a

family, you ought to be prepared to spend a bit of time with them."

Gill said he only went on like that because he couldn't bear Mum being better at work than he was. She said, "He can't take it. Men are weaker than women, really." Well, I dunno. Dad used to be good at everything. He never had to work hard, it always came out right for him.

The other really great thing about Mum having an affair was that I had it in my hands like a time bomb or a grenade or something. I could pull the pin and let it go. I could blow up the family! Or I could quietly sit on it, show it to my mum . . . and make my fortune. It was like a weapon. I'd never really thought before about knowledge as being dangerous like that. When you know certain kinds of things, it's like power. It lets you do things you could never have done before. I started thinking about how to ask Mum to put my pocket money up. It would be a start.

"What's wrong with you?" yelled my dad. I think I heard him, but I assumed he was talking to my mum. There was a pause. He got really cross and he bawled, "I said, what's the matter with you, Laurence?" When he said my name I almost jumped out of my chair.

"What?"

"What? Is that the only word you know? Get a grip, will you? What's the matter?"

I looked at my mum. She blushed. She blushed! It was suddenly like it was all out in the open. *I* blushed. My dad was staring at me, scowling away. Then he noticed my mum as red as a tomato and all his anger went and he looked shocked.

Then I started acting stupid. I don't know what was going through my head. I was fed up with keeping it a secret, I wanted to tell someone and it suddenly occurred to me that it didn't matter if I did. I mean, so what? People have affairs all the time. It was a joke!

I leaned across to my mum and I said, "Give us a kiss, Sandra." And I blew her a kiss and winked. It was the wink that did it. It was a long, slow lecherous wink and it served her right.

I didn't mean to. Maybe I was getting messed up with the game and real life, because although I liked thinking about making all that money, it was like the other ways I've had of getting rich—they never work in the end. Listen, she should have had one of her little talks with me. She should have said something. She just left it up to me, and I'm a child still, right? And . . . she shouldn't have hit me.

Suddenly my mum swung forward and slapped me round my face as hard as she could. It went . . . crack! It really hurt. I put my hand to my cheek and it felt red-hot and smooth.

I didn't actually tell, even then. I just said, "You shouldn't have done that," like it was a threat.

Dad jumped up. He was really angry. "Or what?" he yelled. "Or what?"

I ignored him and I said to my mum, "I didn't tell. So

what did you hit me for?" and I nodded at Dad, just so it was clear who I hadn't told.

Everything was very quiet. I could see my dad licking his lips. Then Mum said, "You and Gill better go upstairs. Your dad and I need to talk."

Gill said, "But we haven't finished."

"Just go upstairs for half an hour. Both of you. Go on."

Gill tutted and groaned, but we got up to go. Mum looked at me and said, "Happy?"

We got upstairs, and I made to go into my room, but Gill grabbed hold of me and said, "What's going on? What's *wrong* with you?" I didn't want to, but she made me tell her everything. Afterwards, she thought I was the most stupid person in the whole world. She started to shout at me, which was a bit much after I'd told her everything. It made me incredibly angry, it was so unfair. I screamed and shouted, I was so angry, and I threw her out of my room. Afterwards, I could hear her crying next door.

Of course, I got the little talk *then*. Then she was right up the stairs, my mum, telling me how it wasn't my fault, but it was all too late then, wasn't it? Anyway, she was only saying that, she never believed it. Gill thought it was my fault all right, she never stopped going on about it. Mum and Dad were always saying how it wasn't my fault at all, but even they say I should have spoken to Mum about it first. But I never let it out, did I? I didn't actually say anything about it.

They were down there for ages. We never did get our pudding. After a while, they started shouting. It went on for ages, and then the next night and the next . . . it just kept on.

The thing that gets me is the way it all just fell to pieces. I don't think they even tried. My dad had it coming, actually. He's always been the smart one, the good-looking one, the clever one. He's one of those people, everything they do is perfect . . . it makes you sick. And then when things do go wrong he can't take it! And he's had affairs . . . he admitted it. Can you believe that? Gill heard them talking about it. You know what he said to Gill when she accused him of being a hypocrite? He said, "Yes, but that was just mucking about. Your mother is *in love*."

The day she left he was working in the garden. All along the bottom of the garden there's a long row of poplar trees. He's been on about them for years. He says poplar trees have robbing roots, which is why nothing grows well in our garden—they steal all the goodness out of the soil. You can find the roots just under the surface almost anywhere in our garden. So on this day, the day she left, he started to dig a trench right across the end of the garden to cut through all the roots growing our way.

Mum said she really wanted to stay, but they had to split up, so she gave him the choice and he chose to stay on at the family home. She said it made more sense because he was the one who was going to be spending more time at home, so he was better able to look after us. Gill said he should have stayed away while Mum was moving her stuff out, but instead of doing that he went into the back garden straight after breakfast. He spent the whole day there, digging this trench. Mum was popping in and out with boxes.

You know what? She made me and Gill help. Well, she tried, anyway. Gill just said no and went into town. I did a couple of boxes, and then I went into my room and sat by the window watching Dad dig his trench. He just worked and worked. Gradually he went deeper into the ground.

About lunchtime I opened the window and shouted out at the top of my voice so everyone could hear, "Why don't you do something? Why don't you *stop* her?" I saw him lift his head up and stare at me, but then he just went back on with his spade. By late afternoon you could just see his head poking out of the top, bobbing up and down as he dug.

Mum went about teatime. She said she'd see us tomorrow at her new place for tea.

"It's just up the road, we can see each other whenever we want," she said. Then she drove off to Nigel. Later, Gill came home and we went out to the garden to see Dad. He stood at the bottom of this trench. It was amazing; it was so deep. I hung around by the shed while she put her hand out to him.

"Coming in, Dad?" she said.

"Has she gone?"

"She's gone."

He ignored her hand and pulled himself up a ladder he had down at one end of the trench. He was all streaked with mud. He looked hopeless. Pathetic. I'd have liked to push him back in the bloody trench and fill the earth in on top of him, he was so useless. Me and Gill stood there looking at him.

"Right. Coped with that pretty well, then, didn't I?"

Gill snorted and suddenly all three of us started laughing. He coped! At the bottom of a trench, I mean. Then he put his arms around our backs and we sort of led him back into the house. He looked shattered. Me and Gill made him some tea and then we all watched telly for a while before we went to bed.

Anne Fine

GETTING THE MESSAGE

How did I tell them? How does anybody tell them? It was a mixture of chance, and being up to here with the sheer awfulness of them not having a clue. (I'm not kidding. I don't think it had even crossed their minds.) I was a wreck from walking through our back door every day after school, practically expecting to see their pale, shocked faces raised to mine. Sooner or later, one of life's meddlers was going to take a swing at them with the old wet sock of truth, and come out with a helpful little "I really thought it was time someone told you." After all, most of my friends knew. And after Mr. Heffer had soft-soled his way up behind me at the newsstand while I was flicking through something pretty dubious, I was pretty sure all the staff at school were in on it (and half the dinner ladies, if that strange rumor about

45

Mr. Heffer has any truth to it). I even reckoned Mr. Faroy, the grocer, had guessed, and I'm not sure he even knows quite what we're talking about. So that just left them, really. Mum and Dad.

Like everyone else, though, I kept putting it off. Not just from cowardice, but from not being sure quite what was driving me towards the dread day of reckoning. I wouldn't be surprised if axe murderers have the same problem. They escape undetected from the scene of the crime, and then each knock, each phone ring, causes such a rush of stomach-clenching fear that in the end they realize one day soon they're going to walk into some police station—any police station—and give themselves up, just to be able to stretch out on their hard prison bed, and breathe in peace. Not the best reason for confessing, perhaps. But good enough. And better than some of the others, like wanting to stop your parents making their tired old jokes about gay presenters on the telly, or simply upset them out of childish spite.

And I certainly didn't want to upset mine. I'm very fond of them, I really am. (Go on. Have a good laugh. I'll wait till you're ready.) I think they're both softies, if you want to know. And I'm the light of Mum's life. Even at my age, they're still checking on me all the time. "All right, are you, son?" "Good day at school, sweetheart?" That sort of thing. Not that I'm actually looking for chances to whinge about that animal Parker hurling my sandwiches into the art room clay bin, or Lucy Prescott stalking me down corridors. But, if I wanted to, I could.

But I couldn't tell them this. Each time I geared myself up, I'd get some horror-show vision in my head of how they might take it. You only need half an ear hanging off one side of your head to know how some parents react. Flora knows someone whose mum wailed on for weeks about it all being *her* fault, then threw herself under a bus. That's something nice for Flora's friend to think about all her life. George has a neighbor whose son was banished. Banished! It sounds medieval, but it happened only last year. And I've just read a novel where the father got drunk and cut the little circle of his son's face out of every single family photograph, and dropped the whole lot down the toilet. The poor boy pads along to the bathroom in the middle of the night, and finds a little whirlpool of his own unflushed faces staring up at him. Maybe the author made that story up. I certainly hope so.

And then there's Mick. We met on holiday last summer and mooched around together quite a bit. When his dad won the accumulator at the races, and Mick clapped him on the back, he made a flinchy little face and moved away. I bet a heap Mick wishes he'd kept his trap shut.

So you can see why I kept putting it off. But we couldn't go on forever. I was sick of not being able to do the simplest things, like keep a proper diary, or snap at Grandpa when he makes remarks about the guys who live together on the corner, or leave the books I'm reading lying about.

And that's how I told them. With a book. Not quite the way you'd imagine, but it worked. Mum and I were in

Readerama a few weeks ago, and she was desperate not to let me out of sight because I was carrying most of the shopping. (She didn't trust me not to put it down. Mum's of the view that trailing half a step behind every single shopper in town is a villain just waiting to pounce on their Priceworthy bags, and make off down some dark alley.) "Have you got all the bags? You're supposed to have six," she says to me every two minutes, and I've known her to have breakdowns just from my slipping one half-empty bag inside another without sending her warning letters in triplicate first. She drives me mad. And she has the nerve to claim she feels the same about me when we're in town together. But I still get dragged along, as unpaid porter, whenever Dad's not available. It's my brute strength she's after, not my advice on broccoli versus sweet corn, or red versus green for the new lavatory brush holder or, as on this particular morning, which cookery book to buy for Aunty Sarah's birthday.

"Just take the cheapest," I said. "It's not as if she ever gets round to actually cooking anything out of them, after all. She just flicks through them and then does chicken and chips."

"What if she has it already?"

"Give her the receipt. Then she can bring it back and choose another. That way, *she* gets to be the one whose arms stretch down to the floor."

Mum took the hint. "All right," she said unwillingly. "You can put down the shopping. But don't move away from it. Stay where you are."

"So what am I supposed to do?"

"Browse," said my mother. "That's what people do in bookshops. Have a little browse."

I browsed. I browsed a step or so to the left (Health Matters). I browsed a step or so to the right (Feminism). I browsed forward a couple of steps (Family and Society), and back a few steps (Cars and Mechanical). And all the time I swear to God I never let a soul get between me and the shopping bags.

Then I got uppity. I browsed a little further away, past Holiday Guides, and round the back of Stamp Collecting. I ended up opposite Food and Drink and, copping a major glower from Mum, who was still choosing which of the eight million cookery books on display Aunty Sarah wouldn't change first, I doubled back through Computers.

Fetching up back at Health Matters, where I'd begun.

That's when I saw it. *Telling Your Parents: A Teenager's Guide to Coming Out in the Family.* You'd think the fairies might have put it there for me. I didn't do what you'd expect—slip it out and have a quick read while she was busy comparing *Feasts of Malaysia* with *You and Your Wok*, then creep back a few days later to read the rest. No. I simply took it off the shelf and tucked it under my arm. Then I dribbled the shopping bags one by one over to Mum at Gluttons' Corner, and stood there growing a beard down to my feet until she'd chosen.

"Right!" she said finally. "I think this one's nice. She can't complain about this one."

She waited for me to point out that Aunty Sarah can complain about anything. But I had bigger fish to fry.

I trailed her to the pay desk.

"Here," she said, taking out her credit card and putting *Winter Cookery: A Casserole Lover's Collection* down on the counter.

"Here," I said, laying *Telling Your Parents: A Teenager's Guide to Coming Out in the Family* straight down on top of it.

"What's that?"

"A book."

"What book?" she said, playing for time as if she couldn't read.

"This book," I said to her firmly. "This book here."

"Take it away, Gregory!" Her voice had shot up in the stratosphere. She was positively squeaking. And the poor girl at the pay desk didn't know where to look. (Would I have done it if it had been a bloke on duty that morning? Don't ask. I'll never know.)

"I mean it, Gregory!" Her hand shot out. The book went sailing off the desk onto the floor. "I'm not buying that for you!"

I felt so sorry for her. But still I picked it up again and put it down on top of *Winter Cookery*.

"No, Gregory! No!" She swiped it off again.

I picked it up. "Come on, Mum."

Snatching it from me, she hurled it on the table to the side of the till. "No! *No!*"

"Yes, Mum," I said, picking it up a third time.

"Oh, no! Oh, no! Oh, God, Gregory!" She reached for the book, but this time the salesgirl dived forward at the same time, maybe to pitch in on my side, maybe to save the book from yet another battering. When their hands met, the book slid off again on to the floor, falling open at a sec-tion called "Telling the Grandparents."

"Oh, God!" she wailed. "I can't believe this is happen-ing!" And I knew from the way it came out that the first of a thousand battles was over. Mum at least believed me.

I've never felt so dreadful in my life. I wanted to say "I'm sorry," but I was worried she'd misunderstand, and get me wrong about the way I feel. So I said nothing. I just stood there like a giant lump, watching my own mum crumple, thanks to me.

Staff training at Readerama must be brilliant. Not only can the sales force read upside down, but they know what to do at sticky moments. Glancing at the name on Mum's card, the girl said gently, "Mrs. Fisher, would you like to come through to the back and sit down for a moment? I could make you some coffee."

Good thing it was my mum I'd dumped the news flash on, and not my dad. He'd have dissolved into a puddle of tears and sat there for a week, weeping into his coffee cup. Mum's made of sterner stuff. She's kept her chin up through some moments of high embarrassment while raising me, and though this must have been about the worst, she still proved equal to the strain.

"That's very nice of you," she said, pulling her coat straight and clutching her handbag closer. "Most kind and thoughtful. But I'll be all right."

The girl gave me a look, and pointed to one of those little stool things they use for getting to the upper shelves. I fetched it over. "At least sit down," she said to Mum. "Just for a moment."

"Just while you ring up the books, then," Mum said, collapsing.

"Books," not "book." Did you notice? I did. So did the girl.

"It won't take a moment," she said. But then she made a point of taking her time, sliding the card through the machine the wrong way once or twice, and rooting underneath the counter for a different-sized bag, to give my mum a few moments. She even came out from behind the pay desk with the slip, and brought it over for Mum to sign. Mum's hand was shaking, but the signature looked close enough to the one on the card.

"There," said the girl, managing to make it sound like "There, there . . ." and making me vow to never in my life buy any book in any shop on the planet but Readerama.

Mum raised her head. "Well, Gregory. We can't stay here all day. Better get home."

And tell your dad, she might as well have added. But I wasn't quite so worried about that. Dad has a flaming temper, but in the end he always buys Mum's line on everything. He wasn't going to like it. Well, who would? Like anyone else, he'd like his son to grow up and marry and have a couple of kids, and not be different in any way. Not because the only thing he cares about is my being "normal," but more because he's quite sure that being different—especially this way—is going to make absolutely everything in my life a whole lot more difficult for me. Once he's convinced this is the only way I'm going to be, he'll get a grip. I'm sure he'll want me happy more than he'll want me straight. I'm lucky there. Some people want you straight a whole lot more than they want you happy.

The bus ride home was pretty quiet (if you don't count Mum saying, "Gregory, have you got all the bags?" two dozen times). Once or twice, she touched my hand, as if she were about to say something. But it was not till we were walking into our own street that she came out with it.

"Let's not say anything about all this just for the moment."

I gave her a suspicious look. What was she thinking? I wasn't old enough to know my mind? That this was something I was trying on, like some new style, or haircut? Did she think I was temporarily unhinged? Under someone's spell? Totally mistaken?

"Just for the moment," she repeated. "Just till we're sure."

No point in climbing out of a box if you're going to climb straight back in again. "I am sure, Mum. I've been sure for years now."

"Well, waiting a little longer before you tell your father won't hurt, then, will it?"

"Mum," I said, "give me one good reason not to tell him now."

She looked quite hunted. "You know how upset he's going to be, and we can't have him saying anything in front of Granny and Grandpa."

Whoa, there! I stopped in my tracks. "And why not?"

She stopped as well. "Gregory, you know perfectly well why not."

I put down the shopping, all six bags of it. "Mum, you can't pick and choose who I keep this secret from," I told her. "It's too important. That has to be *my* decision."

"But what if your grandpa finds out?"

"It's not a matter of him 'finding out,' " I said. "Somebody has to tell him. Otherwise I'll be back exactly where I was before, having to watch myself all the time."

"Is that so terrible?"

"Yes, it is!" I snapped. "And it won't stop there, either. Within a week or so, you and Dad will be trying to kid yourselves it was all just a horrible mistake. No, I'm sorry, Mum. I'm not going back and it isn't fair to ask me."

"Fair?" she snapped, striding off down the street again. "*Fair?* And what about what's fair on the rest of us? You'll give your grandpa a heart attack!"

I'd got her there. "Oh, I don't think so," I said, picking up everything and trailing after her. "Didn't he go ballistic when you told him that Ginny was pregnant by Wayne Poster? And Gran cried for *weeks*. They were so upset and furious, they didn't even go to the wedding. And now look at them! Gran spends her whole life tangled up in pink knitting wool, and Grandpa won't put the baby down. They're tough. They'll get over it."

Mum strode on furiously. "Don't kid yourself they're going to come to terms with this quite so easily!"

"I don't see why not," I said sullenly. "They've got used to my terrible hair. And my terrible clothes. And my terrible music. And my terrible friends. And my—"

"Gregory! This is a whole lot more important than any of those!"

"Yes!" I yelled back. "It certainly is! And that's exactly why I can't go on pretending all the time—not at school, and on the team, and with girls, and at home, and at my Saturday jobs, and *everywhere*. There's got to be *somewhere* I can just be me."

Perhaps I'd got through to her. Or perhaps it was because we'd practically reached our own gate. But, suddenly, she seemed to soften a little. "But surely waiting a little is only sensible. What if you change your mind?"

If this had been school debate, I'd have come back at her pretty sharpish on that one, saying something like "I don't recall you ever saying that you put off marrying Dad in case you found out later that you were lesbian." But this is my mum, don't forget. If I'd said that, she would have slapped me so hard I'd have gone reeling into Mr. Skelley's hedge. So I said nothing.

She peered in my face. "Oh, Gregory. This is going to take a whole lot of getting used to, and I can tell you one thing. The worst isn't over."

"It is for me," I told her quite truthfully.

And what if I did mean the lying, the secrets, the worrying, the pretending? Give me a break! She thought I meant that telling her had been the hardest thing. And that was important to her, you could tell. Shocked and upset as she was, you could still see she took it as a compliment that she mattered most. She took it seriously, the same way she took my blotchy finger painting from nursery, and my cracked jewelry pot from primary school, and my split, wobbly stock cube dispenser from secondary school woodwork class. Her mouth even twitched a little, as if, if she didn't have to go in there and help me through Round Two with Dad, she might even have given me the tiniest of encouraging smiles.

I pushed the gate open. "Ready?" I said, the same way she always used to say it to me when I was starting at a new school or a new club.

"I suppose so," she muttered, exactly the same way I must have said it to her so many times before.

On our way up the path, she suddenly stopped and hurled herself into one of my shopping bags. Scattering socks and lightbulbs, she dragged out *Telling Your Parents: A Teenager's Guide*, and hurried off round the side of the house.

I set off in pursuit. "What are you doing?"

"Stuffing this in the dustbin."

"What, my book?"

But it was already gone, deep under tea leaves and old carrot peelings.

"It's not your book," she said, slamming the lid down over the horrid mess. "It's my book. I'm the one who paid for it." She brushed tea leaves off her hands and added bitterly, "Though I can't think why. You seem to be managing perfectly well without it."

"But why shove it in the dustbin?"

"Listen, young man," she warned me dangerously. "Don't push your luck. If you're planning on making me *live* the bloody book, I'll be damned if I'll dust it."

I know when a job's done. I just picked up the shopping and followed her in to face more of the music.

Sue Limb

YOU'RE A LEGEND

"I'm sorry, Jess—I've got a migraine. You'll have to go on your own."

"NO! No way, Mum!" Jess glared at her mum's rumpled bed. "I am NOT going on my own! I've been totally dreading it anyway. We can go next weekend instead."

"No, we can't," croaked Mum in her headache voice, rasping like something from a horror film. "I've got a librarians' conference next weekend."

"Well, the weekend after, then."

"Daddy's coming to visit then. And we can't keep putting it off. Granny's desperate to get it all sorted. It has to be now. Get me a glass of water, would you please, darling?"

Jess fetched the glass of water. She knew the migraine routine by heart. Her mum would be out of action for twenty-four hours minimum—possibly the whole week-end. She sat down on the bed.

"Thanks," said Mum, sipping the water gratefully. Then she seized Jess's hand in tragic deathbed style. "All you have to do is get the number seventy-three bus to the station, then the Bristol train," she said. "It's the second stop, I think—or, wait, no . . ."

"I know how to get there!" snapped Jess. "I've been there before on my own. Loads of times."

"Right. Of course you have. Sorry," said Mum. "I'm really sorry, Jess. I know it isn't going to be easy, but I'll make it up to you. I promise."

Jess got up off the bed grumpily and slouched off down-stairs. How could her mum possibly make it up to her? She was a poverty-stricken librarian. She simply didn't have ac-cess to the Hollywood lifestyle Jess craved.

The phone rang. Jess grabbed it. *Please, God,* she thought, *make it Granny phoning to cancel because she's ill too.* Instantly she felt guilty at the thought of her beloved Granny being ill. *No, wait, God, let's rethink this.* Jess whizzed off another prayer. *Let Granny cancel because she's feeling well. So well she's off on a fabulous date with a groovy old guy called Max.*

"Hello?" said Jess, picking up.

"Hi, Jess! This is Jodie. I'm having a spur-of-the-moment party tonight. In my uncle's huge garage out at Meadway. Whizzer's DJ-ing. Can you come?"

"No," Jess said, sighing. "This sucks, but I have to do something else."

"What could be more fun than my party?" complained Jodie in her usual bulldozing style.

"I'll tell you what could be more fun," said Jess, letting rip some pent-up aggravation. "Going to stay with my granny all weekend in her grim old house that smells weird, in order to help her sort through my dead grandpa's clothes and stuff. We're going to take it all to the charity shop whilst weeping copiously in stereo. Beat that, you sad disco addict."

Jodie was silent for a moment.

"OK, right," she said eventually. "I'm really, like, sorry and stuff. Hope it goes OK. See you on Monday." She rang off.

Jess slammed down the phone and heaved such a huge sigh that the windows almost rattled. OK, she loved Granny. But it wasn't her job to help sad, old people through all this grieving stuff. She ought to be over at Jodie's party tonight, blinded and deafened by Whizzer's lights and sounds. She was a teenager, for God's sake, not some kind of care worker.

On the train, she closed her eyes, and had a daydream about a poet who had recently come to school to give a talk about his work. His name was Eddie Sadat and he had dark, smoldering eyes, thick, black shiny hair and a cute little mustache. Jess imagined a life with Eddie. They lived in New York, dressed in black and even had matching black Labradors called Darkness and Night.

Eventually, as the train began to slow towards Granny's

station, Jess opened her eyes and stared at her reflection in the train window. She had to accept that her glamorous life with Eddie was never going to happen. The nearest she was going to get to Eddie was growing a similar mustache. In fact, judging by her reflection, that little project was already under way.

However, the daydream did give Jess an idea for getting through this weekend. In every little spare bit of time, she'd design a whole new look for herself. Her normal jeans and trainers outfit was so utterly boring. The idea of slouching stylishly around New York dressed entirely in black had taken her fancy. She had to invent a new look that was cool and wild.

The train stopped. Jess got off and met Granny by the ticket barrier. She seemed smaller than ever and smelled faintly of lavender.

"The taxi driver looks a bit like a mass murderer," whispered Granny excitedly. This was reassuring. They climbed in. The taxi driver seemed a perfectly pleasant fellow with a big smile and crinkly laugh lines round his eyes. But maybe Granny was right; she'd had a lifelong interest in homicide.

The taxi deposited them at Granny's house. Granny seemed a bit disappointed not to have been murdered, but gave the guy a massive tip anyway.

"He knows where we live now," whispered Granny as she unlocked the door and the cab sped away. "I expect he'll be back tonight with his hammer." Not many grannies were so hooked on thrillers. Most other grans tended to be reassuring; Jess's granny was downright irresponsible at times.

"A hammer? Hmm, so crude," said Jess. "I'd rather be shot. Much more stylish."

"Oh, I do agree, dear," said Granny, as they took their coats off. "Now, how about a hot chocolate? I've got one of those pizzas you like—the one with garlic mushrooms and marzipanone."

"Mascarpone," corrected Jess.

"Oh, I love that word!" said Granny. "It sounds like a gangster, doesn't it? Al Mascarpone."

They sat down to lunch and Jess consumed approximately ten thousand calories, after which she began to feel a bit better. But after the washing-up, Granny's mood changed.

"I suppose we'd better start on it," she said with a sigh. "What do you think? We could go at it for a couple of hours, then watch *Pulp Fiction* for a bit of light relief."

"OK, fine," said Jess, though her heart was sinking fast. She'd been dreading this moment. Absolutely dreading it. Maybe Granny would burst into tears. What then? Granny led the way upstairs and into her bedroom. Then she sat down on the bed and sighed.

"Open his wardrobe, dear," she said. Beside the big wardrobe was a much smaller one, which Jess towered over. And this tiny but sinister cupboard was where Jess's grandpa had kept all his clothes. He had died six months ago and Granny had told Mum she hadn't been able to open the cupboard since.

Glamorous way to spend the weekend, thought Jess. She hesitated for a moment and then opened the cupboard. Thank God it was daylight. If it had been dark, Grandpa's ghost might have come swooping out like a sudden gust of dark, tobacco-scented air.

Nothing like that happened. There were just some suits hanging there, and an old camel-colored jacket. It all smelled a bit fusty.

"So all this is going to the charity shop, right, Granny?" asked Jess. She was poised to sweep the whole lot off their hangers and into bin liners.

"Yes—no, wait!" said Granny, looking a bit emotional. Her lip quivered. "That jacket—give it here a minute." Jess passed the camel-colored jacket to her, and Granny sort of fondled it tenderly for a minute.

Please, God, thought Jess urgently, *make her not hug or kiss it. Please!* Granny went through the pockets. She found a couple of coins, a hankie and a lottery ticket. The hankie was crumpled and definitely not clean. Jess wondered if there were any of Grandpa's old bogies hiding within it and if so, whether Granny would put them in a locket and wear them round her neck. A huge bubble of emotion swelled up behind Jess's throat. She was moments away from uttering a tortured scream—or maybe a hysterical laugh.

"Do you think that's a winning lottery ticket?" said Jess. "Grandpa's last stroke of genius." Immediately she wished she hadn't used the word *stroke*. It was a stroke that had caused Grandpa's death.

"He was hopeless at the lottery," said Granny, smoothing the ticket out. "This ticket's past its cut-off date, anyway. And in any case, I'd rather have him back here for just five minutes than all the money in the world."

Suddenly, disastrously, a tear burst from Granny's right eye and ran down her withered old cheek. Jess felt an unbearable urge to run away. She *so* didn't want to get old like Granny. The wrinkles, the funny little bits of skin hanging down below her chin, and the awful sadness . . .

At this most tactless moment, her mobile phone played a vulgar little pinging riff to indicate a text message had arrived.

"Excuse me a minute, Granny," said Jess, diving for the phone. The text was from her best mate, Flora. SO WISH U WERE COMING 2 JODIE'S PARTY, said the text. CAN'T DECIDE WHAT 2 WEAR. WHADDAYA FINK? TART OR GYPSY?

TART EVERY TIME, Jess texted back.

Within seconds Flora had replied to her reply. BTW, TIFFANY SAID HER BRO JACK ASKED IF YOU'D BE THERE! Hastily Jess composed a reply. THANK GOD I'M GLAMOROUSLY ABSENT THEN. GOTTA GO—GRANNY IN TEARS.

She whizzed off the text and switched off her mobile, though it was agonizing to sever her link with her world of tarty togs and torrid parties. Now she had to sink back into the gray and weary world of old age and bereavement. She sat down on the bed and put her arm round Granny. She really did love her. She just wished she wasn't a sad old lady.

Granny blew her nose loudly on Grandpa's hankie, then tucked it away in her sleeve.

"Sorry, dear," she said. "That sounded a bit like an elephant. I've reached a decision. I can't bear to part with all this stuff yet after all. I'm not quite ready. But I do want it out of sight. I'd like to put it all in bags and take it upstairs to the loft. Could you manage to climb up there with the stepladder?"

"Of course!" said Jess. She was relieved that Granny had decided to shelve this project. Quickly she bundled all Grandpa's old clothes into the bin liners. Then she fetched the stepladder from downstairs. It hardly weighed anything at all. Granny kind of faffed around saying things like "Oh, you're so strong, lovey, you're so wonderful," which made Jess feel like some kind of Olympic athlete (for the one and only time in her life, no doubt).

They set up the stepladder under the access to the loft space—a sort of hatch thing in the landing ceiling. Jess reached up and gingerly raised the cover, then climbed up to the very top of the ladder and groped around in the dark. Her head and shoulders were now actually in the attic.

"There's a light switch somewhere on your left," said

Granny. Jess found it and switched on the light. The attic was full of stuff: books, cardboard boxes, old toys, china, general junk . . . and clothes.

"This is amazing!" Jess called down to Granny. "I haven't been up here since I was little."

"If you come back down, dear," said Granny, "I'll pass these bags up to you."

Jess descended a few steps down the ladder, took the bin liners from Granny and hauled them one by one into the attic.

Then Jess looked around more carefully. Some dress-up clothes were hanging from a rail. She remembered them from when she was little. Psychedelic sixties dresses, suede jackets with cowboy fringe . . . all sorts of weird stuff.

"Do you mind if I stay up here for five minutes, Granny?" called Jess. "It's like Aladdin's cave up here and I might find some treasures."

"OK, dear," called Granny. "I'll go and put the kettle on. Be very careful when you come back down."

Jess looked at the clothes again. Was there anything here that could inspire her new wild look? There was a Chinese dressing gown with embroidered dragons on it. Jess tried it on. Unfortunately there wasn't a mirror in the attic, but Jess could tell that she looked fabulously charismatic and could probably charge ten quid for a tarot reading in this gear. However, it wasn't exactly what she was looking for.

She tried on the fringed suede jacket. She felt a bit like an idiot cowgirl and besides, it had started to smell rather manky. In fact, as Jess went through all the other clothes, she noticed that a lot of stuff had been nibbled by mice and moths. And so much of it was in fabrics that were too flashy: gold lurex and pink Lycra. It was a shame.

Then she saw a stack of magazines. Wonderful old magazines from forty years ago! Jess blew the dust off them and sat down on a little old stool to leaf through them. She found miniskirts galore, men with floral ties and hair down to their shoulders, models wearing purple velvet pants and shiny green platform-heeled boots. It was all quite wonderful, but totally useless. Far too pantomime.

She looked round the dusty loft and sighed. Maybe she should go downstairs now and have a cuppa with Granny. She got up and, as she clambered her way back towards the hatch, something caught her eye. It was the front page of an old newspaper, lying on the floor. The headline was: *Mods and rockers clash in Brighton*.

And right below the headline was a photo of a magnificent girl. She was wearing a leather jacket, a denim miniskirt, fishnet tights and motorcycle boots. Her hair was wild and tousled, her lips were set in a sneery pout and her eyes were lined in heavy black.

"Wow!" said Jess aloud. "Jackpot! This is it!" Carefully she picked up the newspaper and blew the dust off it. Now she could see more detail. The girl was wrestling with police officers. In the background was a rather tasty young man, also in black leather, also oozing sex appeal whilst resisting arrest.

This was it! Jess had found her look. And it was going to be easy. You could pick up a black leather jacket for next to nothing in a charity shop. She already had a denim miniskirt, and black fishnet tights were a brief shopping trip away. OK, she might have to save up for the biker boots, but so what? It was *so exactly* the look for her: rugged and wild, but immensely cool.

She tucked the newspaper under her arm, climbed down out of the attic and went downstairs. Granny was sitting watching the TV news, looking rather disappointed.

"It's all about the economic summit," she said. "There haven't been any murders at all. There's a cup of tea in the pot, dear. Would you like a piece of toast?"

"In a minute, Granny," said Jess. "I just want to show you something I found in the attic."

"What, dear?" asked Granny. "A treasure?"

"Well, yes, in a way," said Jess. "Do you know, Granny, I've been trying to work out a new look for myself. You know, I look like a hobo most of the time."

"I think you look lovely, dear," said Granny. Well, of course she would. But looking "lovely" according to your granny is hardly going to be cool, is it?

"Thanks, Granny, but I want a change," said Jess. "And I found this fantastic photo in an old newspaper up there. . . ." She opened out the folded newspaper and showed Granny the front page. "Look at her!" said Jess. "She's just amazing, isn't she? I mean, not because she's being arrested or anything . . ." (Jess didn't want Granny to panic that she was choosing deviant role models.) "She's just, well, amazing," said Jess, leaning back and staring in admiration at the feisty and furious girl rocker. Granny looked at the picture and smiled nostalgically.

"Ah, yes," she said. "The Whitsun Weekend, 1964. I remember every minute. Glad you approve."

"Approve?" said Jess, not quite following Granny's drift.

"It's the only time I've ever made the front page," said Granny with a proud sigh.

"What?" gasped Jess. "You mean that's *you?*"

"I'm afraid so, dear," said Granny. "I was arrested because I sort of lost it, as they say, when they arrested Grandpa."

"They arrested *Grandpa?*" shrieked Jess.

"Well, he was attacked by three mods, dear, and he sort of lashed out, you know. We were rockers, you see. We rode about on motorbikes and we liked Elvis. The mods had silly little scooters and they were all a bit soft. Sort of wimps, they seemed like, to us."

Jess stared in total astonishment at the photo. So this iconic girl, with the wild hair and the blazing eyes, in the leather and boots, was her *Granny?* It scarcely seemed possible.

"How old were you?" she asked.

"Oh, about nineteen," said Granny dreamily. "My dad

69

was furious. But although we were arrested, we weren't charged. Ah! Those were the days. Elvis's 'Jailhouse Rock' was our tune, but it didn't turn out to be spookily appropriate, thank God!"

As she stared at the photo of her younger self, Granny's eyes danced at the memory of that seaside punch-up long ago. Jess was amazed. Slowly it was dawning on her. She wasn't spending the weekend with a wrinkly, bereaved old lady. She was spending it with a magnificent girl biker, who rode motorbikes, wrestled with police officers and blazed out triumphantly from the front pages of newspapers.

"Right," said Granny briskly. "I'll just make you some toast, and fresh tea, I think, and then, how about *Pulp Fiction* for the fortieth time?"

"Granny," said Jess, "you're a legend." And she wasn't kidding.

Jacqueline Wilson

THE BAD SISTER

It's a beautiful gravestone. A little girl angel spreads her wings, head shyly lowered, with neat stone curls never in need of brushing. Her robe is ornately tucked and gathered, a little fancy for an angel frock, as if she's about to attend a heavenly party.

I step over the miniature rosebush and feel along the carving on the gravestone with one finger. I whisper the name.

Angela Robinson.
(My name.)
Beloved Daughter.
(Not me.)
Born 1984. Died 1991.

My sister. She died in 1991. I was born in 1992, eleven months later. Another Angela, to replace the first. I suppose that was the theory. Only it hasn't worked out that way. I'm not a little angel.

I reach out and slap the gravestone angel hard on her perky little nose. She smiles serenely back at me, above retaliation. I hit her harder, wanting to push her right off her pedestal. A woman tending a nearby grave looks up, startled. I blush and pretend to be buffing up the angel's cheeks with the palm of my hand.

I haven't been here for a while. Mum used to bring me week in, week out, every single Sunday when I was little. I brought my Barbie dolls and some scraps of black velvet and played funerals. My prettiest bride Barbie got to be Angela. I sometimes pinned tissue wings on her and made her flap through the air in holy splendor.

One time, I dressed her in a nightie and wrapped her up in a plastic carrier bag and started to dig a little hole, all set to bury her. Mum turned round from tidying Angela's flowers and was appalled.

"You can't dig here. This is a cemetery!" she said.

The cemetery seemed a place purpose-built for digging, though I knew enough not to point this out. Mum was going through a bad patch. Sometimes she seemed normal, like anyone else's mum, *my* mum. Then she'd suddenly burst into tears and start a crying spell.

I was always frightened by her tears. There was nothing

decorous about her grief. Her eyes were bleary and blood-shot, her face damp and greasy, her mouth almost comically square. I'd try putting my arms round her. She didn't ever push me away, but she didn't always gather me up and rock me. Sometimes she scarcely seemed to notice I was there.

She still has crying spells now, even though Angela has been dead for fifteen years. I'll invite Vicky or Sarah home from school and we'll discover Mum crying in the kitchen, head half hidden in the dish towel. Birthdays are bad times too. And Christmas is the worst. Angela died in December. A quick dash . . . an icy road . . . a car that couldn't brake in time.

One Christmas, Mum got so crazy she bought two sets of presents. One pile of parcels for me, one for my dead sister. I don't know how Mum thought she was going to give the first Angela her presents. She could hardly lob them right up to heaven. I imagined Angela up on her cloud, playing with her big blue teddy and her Little Mermaid doll and her giant rainbow set of felt-tip pens.

After a few weeks my own teddy's plush was matted, I'd given my Little Mermaid doll an unflattering haircut, and I'd pressed too hard on my favorite purple pen so that it wouldn't color neatly anymore. The first Angela would have looked after her presents.

The first Angela didn't leave the bath tap running so that there was a flood and the kitchen ceiling fell down. The first Angela didn't get into fights at school and poke

73

out her tongue at the teacher. The first Angela didn't bite her nails, tell fibs or wet the bed.

My grandma would actually tell me to ask Angela for help, as if she'd already acquired saintly status.

"Pray to your sister to help you stop having temper tantrums. Ask Angela for advice on how to stop biting your nails. See if Angela can help you with wetting the bed—your poor mother can't cope with all the extra laundry."

Dad was furious when he found out, and he and Gran had a big row. Then Mum and Dad argued too, and for a little while Dad wouldn't let me see Grandma anymore. We didn't often see my other gran or any of Dad's family—I think someone had said something tactless about my name way back at my christening and Mum wouldn't speak to them again.

We're still not on very friendly terms with that side of the family—so it was a surprise when the wedding invitation came through the letter box this morning. Mum opened it and stared, fingering the deckle edge.

"What is it?" I asked.

"Nothing," said Mum. She tried to crumple it up, but it was too stiff.

Dad looked up from his newspaper.

"Is that a wedding invitation?" he said. "Let's have a look."

"It's nothing," Mum repeated, but Dad reached across and snatched it from her.

"Good lord! Becky's getting married," said Dad.

"My cousin Becky?" I said. "Is she the one who used to be best friends with Angela?"

Dad usually frowns at me when I mention the first Angela, because he doesn't want to set Mum off—but now he just nodded.

"And we're invited to the wedding?" I said. I got up and peered over Dad's shoulder. "To the ceremony. And the wedding breakfast. Doesn't that sound weird? It's not a real breakfast, like bacon and egg, is it? And a disco in the evening. So . . . are we going?"

"I don't think so," said Mum.

"I think we ought to go," said Dad.

"You go if you want. But I don't think I can face it," said Mum, rubbing her eyebrows with her thumb and forefinger, the way she always does when she has a headache. "Angela and Becky were just like sisters."

"So why shouldn't we see Becky married?" Dad said. "I've hated the way we've barely seen the family all these years. I know it's painful, I know it brings back memories— but life goes *on*. It's not fair to me to cut me off from my family. And it's not fair to Angela either."

"Not fair to *Angela?*" said Mum. It took her a second to realize he meant me.

"I don't *want* to go to Becky's wedding," I said.

I didn't want all the family looking at me, shaking their heads, whispering. I was sure they'd all compare me with the first Angela. I knew they'd say I wasn't a bit like her.

"There," said Mum. "That settles it." But she looked

doubtful. She picked up her teacup, but then put it down without a sip. The cup clattered in the saucer. It was obvious her hand was trembling.

"We'll all go," Dad said firmly.

"Oh please, don't, both of you," I said, getting up from the table. "I'm going to school."

I rushed off before I could get caught up in the argument. I tried to forget about it at school. I mucked around with Vicky and Sarah, I got told off for talking in class, I got the giggles in singing, I played the fool on the hockey pitch doing a sword dance with my hockey stick, I wrote a very rude but very funny joke on the toilet wall—while Angela hovered above my head, her wings creating a cold breeze.

I didn't get the bus home with Vicky and Sarah. I walked right through the town and out to the cemetery instead.

I don't know why.

Maybe I want to talk to Angela. And yet here I am assaulting her, slapping her stone angel around.

"I'm sorry," I whisper, and I reach out and hold the angel's hand. Her fist stays clenched. She wouldn't want to hold hands with me. The bad sister.

I'm very late home. Mum is at the window, white-faced. She's already phoned Dad and he's come rushing home from work.

"Where have you *been?*" Mum says, bursting into tears.

"How could you be so thoughtless?" says Dad.

Mum can't bear me being even ten minutes late, because she's so scared there will have been another accident.

"I'm sorry, I'm sorry, I'm *sorry*," I gabble. "Look, I went to the cemetery, OK?"

"Oh, darling," says Mum. She gives me a hug.

Even Dad looks sheepish.

I feel guiltier than ever. They think I'm so devoted to my dead sister. They have no idea I sometimes can't stand her.

"Let's have tea," says Mum.

"What's happening about Becky's wedding?"

"We needn't go. I'll write a note to explain—and we'll send her a nice present," says Dad.

"Well. Maybe we *should* go. I think I was being a bit . . . selfish," says Mum. "We should wish Becky well. Angela— you know, *Angela*—she'd have wanted to go, wouldn't she? And it's right, we have this Angela, *our* Angela, to think of."

"But," I said, "I don't want to go."

It doesn't matter what I say. We're going. And that's that. Dad phones his sister. Mum writes an acceptance note. Dad buys a crystal decanter and glasses as a wedding gift. Mum chooses a new suit, blue with a black trim.

"You'll have to have a dress, Angela."

"*Me?*" When I'm out of school uniform I live in jeans and T-shirts.

"Come on now, Angela, use your head," Mum says

impatiently. "You can't go to a wedding in trousers and trainers."

She drags me all round this grim department store looking at the most terrible outfits. I moan and complain. Eventually we fetch up in Topshop and I get a dress and a purple jacket and new shoes. I get quite excited at the way I look. Older, for a start, and although the shoes pinch like hell, it's really cool to be wearing sexy high heels.

"You look lovely, Angela," says Dad, when I dress up. I *feel* lovely too.

Not on the wedding day, though. My hair won't go right, for a start. It sticks out in a terrible frizz and won't be subdued. I've got little spots on my forehead and chin and I slap on so much makeup to cover them that it looks like I'm wearing a beige mask. I have to wash it off and start all over again. I splash water on my dress and I'm scared it will mark. I'm not sure it really goes with the jacket now. My shoes are still beautiful, but whenever I try to walk I go over on my ankle.

I'm going to look a right sight at the wedding. I stare at myself in the mirror. The first Angela peeps over my shoulder, her fine eyebrows raised.

Mum's having second thoughts too. When we set off, her eyes are red and her nose is shiny and she clutches her lace hankie as if it's a cuddle blanket. Dad puts his arm round her and gives her a quick squeeze.

Everyone stares at us when we get to the church. People hang back as if our stale mourning is contagious, but then my aunt gives my dad a hug and soon everyone's whispering and waving and Mum manages to smile bravely and wave back. I keep my head down, glancing up under my bangs every now and then at all these relations who are practically strangers. I haven't got a clue who half the people are.

There's a good-looking lanky guy with dark hair who peers round at me curiously. He's wearing a shirt the exact royal purple of my jacket. He grins, acknowledging this. I grin back foolishly. And then the organ music starts up and Becky and my uncle come walking down the aisle.

The guy keeps looking at me during the ceremony and the reception. (I'm allowed my very first glass of champagne.)

He doesn't come and talk until the disco starts. He stands behind my chair, fingering the jacket I've slung over the back.

"Snap," he says.

"Snap," I reply, casually.

"Would you like to dance?"

Would I! Though the glass of champagne and my new high heels make me walk very warily onto the dance floor. He is really gorgeous and he's asked *me* to dance. He's quite a bit older than me too, probably nineteen or twenty. A student. Smiling at me. I hope he doesn't know I'm only fourteen. I don't think he's family.

"What's your name?" I mumble shyly.

"James. And you're Angela."

"How do you know?"

"Well, I live next door to Becky. I knew your sister."

My heart misses a beat.

"You're not a bit like her," he says.

I knew it.

"Not that I can remember her all that well. I was only a little kid when she . . . But I remember that last summer because she came to stay with Becky. She had all this pretty blond hair and big blue eyes, yes?"

"Like a little angel," I say. I've stopped dancing.

"Mmm," says James. He pauses. "Well. Not exactly *angelic*. I was terrified of her, actually."

"You were . . . what?"

"I was this pathetic little wimp, scared stiff of the big girls. They teased me and I blubbed and that only made them worse."

"My sister, Angela?"

"Becky wasn't too bad, but Angela gave the most terrible Chinese burns. And she had this way of pulling my ears, really twisting them. You're not into ear-twisting, are you?"

I shake my head, still too surprised to joke.

"So Angela really gave you a hard time? I just can't imagine her doing stuff like that."

"No one else could either. Whenever I told on her she batted those blue eyes and looked so sweet and innocent that no one believed me. I'm sorry. Maybe I shouldn't talk about her like that."

"No, no—tell me more," I say, picking up the beat and dancing again.

Up above, sparkling in the strobe lighting, Angela is taking off her halo, folding her feathery wings, little horns sprouting through her blond curls. She's waving her new forked tail at me. My bad sister.

Celia Rees

CALLING THE CATS

In August, the great house had looked benign and beautiful; the honey-colored stone glowing in the sunlight, the banks of leaded windows shiny and square, open to the air. Now the stone was mottled and dull. The casements were fastened tight and all the little panes looked blank and black, as if the house was filled with darkness. The gates were now closed with a computer-printed notice cased in plastic and taped to the bars: *Open again April 5th.* The house had only been shut for a month or so, but moss had begun to coat the carefully raked gravel like velvet. The neat flowerbeds looked ragged, and leaves drifted in heaps across the lawns; the grass was patched with tattered black ink caps and rings of slimy little toadstools.

It hadn't taken long for the house to take on a deserted,

even neglected, air. Jules was cold already; the prospect of living here made her shiver more.

"We're not going to live in *there*," her mum said, peering through the bars with her. "We've got a flat over the stables. All mod cons. Central heating. Furniture from IKEA. You don't even have to go into the old part, if you don't want to."

"But *you* do."

Her mother laughed. "I don't spook as easily as you."

"Yoo-hoo!" They both turned to see a short blond woman, gesticulating at them. "You can't get through that way! Over here!"

They followed her round to the stable yard.

"*This* is where you'll be living." The blonde peered at them. "Didn't they explain?"

"I know," Jules's mother said. "We were just having a look, that's all."

"It's Zadie, isn't it?"

"Sadie," Jules's mother corrected.

"Of course!"

"Nice to meet you again, Monica."

"And this is?" Monica squinted harder, as if screwing up her eyes would help her remember.

"Jules."

"Julie! I remember! You were at school with my Katie!"

"A while ago." Jules scuffed at the yellow gravel. "Yeah."

"Now, Zadie—"

"Sadie."

"Yes." She teetered back on heels a little too high for her rounded frame. "Sorry." Her big red-lipstick smile did not rise to her pale blue eyes. "Is that the time?" She looked over at the church tower. "Here are the keys." She handed Sadie a big bunch. "I'm sure you've been over everything with Derek. Here's my card if you encounter any problems. Must run." She was already stepping backwards towards her car. "I've got a meeting in Cheltenham."

She let out a cry and nearly toppled over as fur brushed the backs of her legs. Jules had to stifle giggles. The cat must have been under her car, but he'd appeared as if from nowhere to rub himself against Monica's substantial calves. He was big, sinuous and long—obviously a tom—with unusual markings: his deep, amber fur thickly barred with black. There was definitely a touch of the Siamese about his narrow face and tilted green eyes.

"That reminds me. You're expected to feed the moggies. I don't know which one this one is. . . ."

"The cat's name is Aloysius," Jules said.

"How do you know that?" Monica asked, astonished.

"When we were here in the summer, one of the guides told me."

"Oh, right."

Monica reached down to stroke him. The cat's ears flicked back, lying flat against his sleek head. He opened his mouth to show long, pointed teeth and let out a sound somewhere between a growl and a hiss. Curved claws, sharp and black, lashed out. Monica snatched her hand away. Blood beaded on her palm, as red as her nail polish.

"Vicious little brute! They're quite wild, as you can see."

"You should get to know his name," Sadie said under her breath. "Maybe he's touchy about it."

"Say what?" Monica looked at her.

Jules felt the giggles breaking like bubbles in her nose, making her eyes sting.

"I just asked if you were all right." Sadie smiled sweetly. "Do you need a Band-Aid? I've got a hankie. . . ."

"No, thank you. A tissue will do." Monica fished one out of her bag to staunch the blood and gave a shaky laugh. "We ought to put a notice up. *Beware of the Cat!*"

Jules used the cover of Monica's feeble joke to let out her smothered laughter. Her mirth died quickly as she thought she caught a movement in one of the upper stories, like someone reaching to open a window. She blinked and . . . there was no one there. Jules smiled as she followed her mother to the stable block. *Definitely* too much imagination.

"Oh, it really is too much!" Lavinia stamped her foot, although the tiny buttoned boot made no sound as it hit the ground. "We should be down there! It's such a bore to be stuck in the house while Aloysius has all the fun." She beckoned the others over, to share the scene below her, and then had to admonish Jessica for getting too close to the window. She was reaching up to open it!

"Don't!" she scolded. "Keep away from the window."

"Why?" Jessica scowled and her rosebud mouth pursed to a sulk. Lavinia was far too bossy. "They can't see us."

"*Some* can," Lavinia replied.

Jessica skipped away to play with the others. "All the more fun!"

Sadie threw the card onto the kitchen counter. "I can't believe she couldn't get our names right. I've known her for years!"

"Is she the one who interviewed you?"

"No, that was Derek. Didn't even know she was working for the National Trust. Last thing I knew, she was volunteering at the local museum. You do think you'll like it here?" she added, changing the subject. "It's just that it's perfect for me to finish the book, and with our house not ready . . ."

After her marriage broke up, Sadie had wanted a complete break. She had accepted a job at Michigan State University, teaching creative writing. Jules had elected to go to America with her. They'd spent a year there and come back in July. Sadie had found a house, but it needed work. They wouldn't be able to move in for months and months.

"We could always go back to Granny's."

"Not another day! Staying with my mother is *not* an

option. She treats me as though I'm still your age." Sadie sighed. "I'll take that as 'I don't like it,' shall I?"

Jules went over and gave her a hug. "No, don't do that. I'm fine with it. It's just a tiny bit creepy." Jules felt an uneasiness she could not define. "The house . . ."

"Is not creepy!" Sadie hugged her daughter back. "Just different with nobody in it. I'll prove it. Come with me."

The wood of the door was weathered silver and opened onto the porch. The Trust had tried to keep a flavor of how the house used to be. It had been owned by an eccentric old lady who had run her own tours: sixpence for children, one shilling for adults.

"Totally batty, by all accounts," Jules's mother commented. "Place was inches thick with dust, and totally infested with cats."

"What happened to her?"

"She got too old to manage the place. Gave it to the Trust. Lives in a nursing home in Cheltenham now. Not far from your old junior school."

They had lived in Cheltenham before the year in America and, although the house was only about twenty miles away from where they used to live, Jules had never visited it before the summer.

"It was shut up for a long while after the old lady moved out; then the Trust were doing it up. Must say, they've done a good job." Sadie sniffed, her nose wrinkling. "Pity they couldn't have done something about the cats."

"Perhaps they come with the house."

They both laughed, although Jules's words were truer than she knew.

It was like the old lady had just stepped out. The hand-painted signs were still there. An old raincoat hung in petrified folds; umbrellas, their cloth tattered like crows' feathers, rusted in a worm-eaten stand; a pair of perished wellington boots lay keeled over in the corner, as if they had tired of waiting for an owner who had walked out years ago and never come back. Pots of geraniums and pelargonium were ranged along the windowsill: a jungle of writhing stems and straggly blooms raining the last of their red petals like showers of blood. They filled the stuffy space with their peppery, lemony scent, and behind that was a strong smell of cats.

"You don't have to come round with me." Sadie sensed her daughter's reluctance as she opened the front door.

"What's that?" A last shaft of sunlight, striking low through the porch windows, showed a circle divided by more circles to make a looping petal pattern scratched into a wooden panel. Jules put out a finger to trace it. "It looks like the hex symbols that we saw in America."

"A witches' sign? Put at the threshold to guard the house?" Sadie bent forward to take a closer look. "Could be. Why does this house need protecting?"

Jules shivered. Sometimes the signs were not to keep something out, but to keep something in.

They continued down the passage into the Great Hall.

It was late in the afternoon and high windows made it as gloomy as a cave in here. The chill room smelled of freshly applied beeswax polish, but underneath that was a distinct, dusty tang of ancient coal fires. The white dust sheets, shrouding the furniture, glimmered in the half-light. Above their heads, the threadbare colors of some long-forgotten regiment stirred and fluttered. The banners were cobweb thin and probably disturbed by their coming in, although the draft of air seemed to come from above, as if the house, or something in it, was stirring, waking to their presence.

Mother and daughter drew closer together.

"I don't think we have to explore any more, do you?" Sadie said. Jules shook her head. "Let's go back to the flat and put the kettle on, shall we?"

Jules settled in reasonably well. The flat was comfortable, the fully modernized conversion tastefully done. She liked her new school and made friends quickly. She would have been quite happy with her new life if it hadn't been for the house. And the cats. She didn't mind cats in general; in fact she quite liked them, or had done until now. She was in charge of feeding them: Aloysius, the big amber tom; a gray female; a white and ginger; a tortoiseshell; and two black ones, the smaller one almost a kitten. They were a vicious crew, milling round, spitting and snarling, tails whipping, ready to start on her when they had finished the

Whiskas. Jules just emptied the cans and ran. They were not allowed in the house, although that prohibition didn't seem to stop them. They had the run of the place.

There had always been cats, Susan, one of the girls on the school bus, said. They went with the house. They'd belonged to the old lady. "They've tried all sorts," she said. "They just come back. She was a bit of an old witch, by all accounts. Maybe she put a spell on them."

Susan laughed, but Jules couldn't see what was funny.

A maze filled one half of the garden. Four paths led through archways and then branched out into a pattern that had been cut into the turf. The paths turned in circles in and out of each other. It was hard to see from ground level, but from Jules's window the pattern looked very like the witch mark scratched on the panel in the hall of the house. A circle of huddled topiary stood at the middle of the maze. Each bush was clipped, but it was impossible to see what the shape had been originally, or what it was meant to be. This was the cats' favorite place. There were always some here, chasing each other, or lying in wait for birds under the odd collection of strange, bulbous shapes.

Jules liked the maze. It wasn't one of those where you couldn't see over the hedges. You didn't need to take a pack of sandwiches in case you got lost, but that didn't make it any less intriguing. The pattern looked simple, but it took a surprisingly long time to walk, and you only got to the middle if you started at the path that led to the little grave-yard and the family chapel.

One particular day, it took longer than usual for Jules to get to the center. The sun had disappeared, sinking below the level of the surrounding hills. Jules looked up, orienteering herself by the bulk of the house to the right and the church to the left, its squat tower just visible through a thick fringe of holly and yew. It felt as though she had traveled a long way.

Down at ground level, eyes stared—every shade from deepest orange to pale yellow. The cats did not run away, as they normally did, but edged nearer, tightening the circle. They walked around, nose to tail, in the most disconcerting way, and then they were gone. Their place was taken by a ring of children with Jules standing in the middle. They began circling round her, moving faster and faster, faster than real children could ever go. Jules began turning with them, *Ring a ring a roses,* the tune started in her head, inconsequentially. Perhaps they had all died of plague. But no, wrong century. These were dressed in the clothes of a hundred years ago or so. Not now, that was for sure.

All fall down!

An older girl dragged them down, left and right, and then stepped over the prone bodies.

"Hello, I'm Lavinia." The girl looked at Jules. The children round her were rising. "This is Jessica, Heather, Fred and little Samuel."

The children all stared. The girls curtsied. The boys bowed.

"That's the way we come." The girl nodded in the direction of the little gate that led into the graveyard. "We're all in there. We come through the troy town." She described the pattern with a thin finger. "That's the old name for the maze. It's been here a long time. Longer than the house. That's how we came back."

Jules tensed, ready to make a break for it. A hand shot out and grabbed her wrist. The girl might be ghostly, ethereal, but she had a grip of steel.

"You can't go yet!" Lavinia said. "We've been looking forward to *playing* with you. We so want for different company. But you have been rather standoffish."

"Thrice the brindled cat hath mew'd . . ." the words came into Jules's head. *Macbeth, Act 4, Scene 1.* They were studying the play at school.

A boy stepped out from behind one of the shapeless, bulbous bushes. He was about twelve or thirteen, with auburn hair a deep shade of amber, and slanted green eyes under brows like thick black bars.

"Here comes Aloysius. He wants you to stay, too. We all do. Well, not *you* so much." Her tone became more confiding. "There are *plenty* of children. What we need is a mummy to look after us."

She lisped her words between tiny teeth, wide-spaced and splayed. She'd be wearing an impressive set of braces if she lived now, Jules thought.

"We *had* a mummy who used to live here," the girl went on, "but she went away."

She must mean the old lady.

"How?" Jules's mouth was so dry, she could hardly get the words out. "How did you get here?"

"There was an accident. Out on the lake. When we were all children." She frowned. "I *told* Aloysius the ice would crack! *She* wouldn't come out with us. Aloysius called her a scaredy-cat!" Lavinia sighed. "We were put in there." She pointed to the lichen-encrusted wall of the graveyard. "*She* grew up, but then she missed us. Her brothers and sisters, and cousin Aloysius. She was lonely, so she called us to her, through the troy town. She called us back. She kept us as cats, but we prefer to be children. She's gone now." Her mouth pouted in momentary sadness, then settled in a thin determined line. "So we need another grown-up to look after us. Someone who *won't* go away. Ever!"

"Soon! Soon!" one of the little ones cooed. "Soon we will have a mummy!"

Lavinia frowned. "Shut up, Sammy!"

Jules didn't stop running until she reached the flat. From the window, she could see darkness at the center of the maze, a pool of shadows taking on shapes, now children, now vague huddled humps like the surrounding topiary. The outlines lost their fuzziness and gathered like inky mist, blacker than the surrounding darkness, forming and re-forming into things malignant and horrible. *We have been here a long time, we will be here forever and you will join us,* the shapes seemed to tell her, before they coalesced into a line of cats and slid off into the graveyard.

Jules was nervous about visiting the graveyard, but she knew that she would have to go. She chose a sunny day when there were no cats about. She found a row of little graves, all with the same date: 21st December, 1929. Jules went back to the kitchen and looked at the calendar. It was halfway through December now. It would happen on the twenty-first. That was the date that they'd chosen, Jules just knew. It marked the solstice, and their special anniversary. That was when they would want their new mother. The only way to get her was to kill her.

Jules had no idea how they would do it, but they were clever and malevolent. They would find ways. Jules didn't go into the great house, but her mother did. The lighting was subdued, so as not to damage delicate wall coverings and fabrics; in some places, in the upper stories, there was no electric light at all. The stairs were tall, twisting and narrow, easy to lose your footing on—tripped by a cat, for example. The road leading to the house was steep—perilous in icy weather, and no gritters came out here. She had to get Mum away. The sooner the better.

Jules went through the possibilities. The truth was not an option. Sadie didn't believe in ghosts. A full-on "I don't like it here" would get a dusty "Neither do I, but we've got to get on with it." She could try: "I hate the school. I'm being bullied." But her report was going to say: "Julia has made lots of friends and fits in well." Anyway, Sadie would say, "See how it goes in the New Year." Except there wouldn't *be* a New Year. Jules could feel their malice accumulating like the fog that crept along the valley. Whatever she did would have to be quick, but every plan she came up with came to nothing, or had a great big hole in it. Even if she and Mum did get away, they weren't too fussy about who was going to be their *mummy;* they'd soon find some-one else. Monica, for example. She'd have to come and feed them. . . . Monica might be all kinds of a cow, but Jules wouldn't wish that on her. And she had a daughter, Katie. . . . No. There had to be another way.

Jules watched from her window, trying to see if there was a pattern in their behavior. They came out as cats in the morning, streaming in a line down the path from the graveyard to be fed. They went back in the evening, dis-appearing through the little gate, tails in the air. A plan began to form in her mind.

Now came the scary bit. Jules steeled herself to do it, following them as closely as she dared, dodging round the hunched humps of the topiary, keeping to the shadows. Their sinuous shapes slithered like eels round the gray wood of the gate. She waited, counting the beats of her heart, giving them time to get "home."

Aloysius. He was the most dangerous. She'd start with him, and then move on to Lavinia. She squatted down above the short oblong, marked out in stone, which contained his bones. Her hand shook as she scratched the circles onto the headstone with a chisel. *Keep them in as well as out*, the words chanted in her head like a mantra. She had no idea if it would work or not, but it was the only magic she knew. When she had finished, she laid a sprig of holly on the moss-encrusted gravel, and went on to the next. Her hand shook even harder as she heard the sound, muffled but loud. A deep-throated yowl rose up from beneath her, strong enough to vibrate the ground. She nearly dropped the chisel and ran, but made herself continue. Aloysius was calling to the others. She had to work fast. The cry was taken up by one, then another; a high-pitched yodeling, an unearthly pleading, somewhere between anguish and anger, halfway between cat and child, in no language known to man. The calling rose in a crescendo as she worked on the last grave, then subsided, the voices dying away one by one, silenced forever. Jules rested back on her heels, her whole body shaking. It was only then that she noticed the gash in her wrist, the blood springing in bright beads, as red as the berries on the sprig of holly that she had just laid on the last grave.

"What are you doing, out here in the dark?"

Jules almost toppled over with shock.

"I was, um, collecting holly," she mumbled as her mother helped her to stand. "For decorations. Deck the halls, and all that."

"What happened to your arm?"

Blood showed against the white of Jules's wrist.

"Brambles. Have you seen these?" She pointed down at the small graves at their feet. "Children. All died in an accident."

"How do you know?" Sadie bent down to look at the inscriptions.

"I just assumed," Jules said hastily. "Because they all died on the same day."

"How tragic! And tomorrow is the anniversary! We ought to do something. How about Christmas roses?" Sadie stood up. "We could plant them by their graves."

"Yes." Jules took her mother's hand. "I think they'd like that."

Malorie Blackman

HUMMING THROUGH MY FINGERS

My hands slowed, then stilled on my book as I listened. I turned my head and sniffed at the wind. Mum always said I had ears like a bat, but if it wasn't for the wind blowing in my direction I doubt if even I would have heard this particular conversation. I listened for a few moments until I'd heard enough, then returned to my book—which was far more interesting. Nine pages on and I was interrupted. I'd thought I'd get at least twelve pages further on before he plucked up the nerve to come over.

"Hi, Amber. It's Kyle. Kyle Bennett." He didn't have to tell me his name. I recognized his voice. Kyle Bennett—the new boy in my brother Matthew's class. Well, when I say new I mean he'd been in Matthew's class for over a month now. Kyle had been to our house once or twice with some of Matt's other friends, but this was the first time he'd actually said anything to me. I sniffed the air. I could smell a lie. Not lies. Just one lie. Even if I hadn't heard, I would've known.

"Can I sit down?"

"I don't know." I shrugged. "Can you?"

"Huh?"

I smiled. A teeny-tiny smile for a teeny-tiny joke.

"No, I . . . er . . . I meant, d'you mind if I sit down?" Kyle's voice was anxious, eager for me to understand.

"Help yourself." I carried on with my book.

"What're you reading? Is it good?"

"*Rebecca* by Daphne du Maurier. And yes, it is good. I've read it before."

"If you've read it before, why're you reading it again?" asked Kyle.

"It's one of my favorites." All the time I spoke I carried on reading, my fingers skimming over the page. But then my fingers unexpectedly touched Kyle's and an electric shock like a bolt of lightning flashed through my fingers and up my arm.

"Ouch!" Kyle exclaimed.

With his touch still humming through my fingers, I snatched my hand away. "Are you OK?"

"Yeah, I just got a shock." Kyle dismissed it easily. I could hear that he was still shaking his sore fingers. "I don't see how we could've been shocked just sitting on grass."

I said nothing. It was there in his touch too. The touch

of a lie. Not a liar, but a lie. But there was something else there. Something that stopped me from telling him to get lost.

"Sorry about that," Kyle said. "I just wanted to see what Braille was like."

"Why?" I could smell his surprise at my question.

"I've never seen a Braille book before. How does it work?"

Here we go again. I sighed. Another explanation. Another embarrassed pause followed by a murmur of sympathy and, under normal circumstances, a sudden mumbled excuse to leave. But these weren't normal circumstances.

"Each of the series of dots represents a letter or number," I explained. "I use my fingers to read the dots rather than my eyes to read the words on a page, that's all."

"Can I have a try?"

"Go ahead."

I picked up the book and held it in Kyle's direction. He took it from me, careful not to touch my fingers this time.

"It must take ages to learn all this lot. It would take me years." Kyle whistled appreciatively. "How long did it take you?"

"Quite a few months," I replied. And I admit, I was surprised. No pity, no sympathy, just two people talking. I like surprises. If only it had been some other boy besides Kyle who had managed to surprise me.

"Were you born blind?"

Another surprise. No one outside my family ever

discussed my eyes—not directly with me, at any rate. It was a taboo subject, conspicuous by its absence. I wondered who else was present, who else was listening? I sniffed the air. I couldn't smell anyone else nearby.

"No." I was going to say more, but the words didn't seem to want to leave my mouth.

"So how did you become blind, then?"

I forced myself to speak. "I'm a diabetic and I'm one of the unlucky few who became blind because of it."

"What d'you miss most?"

"People's faces—and colors." Silence stretched between us as I listened to Kyle search for something else to say. "What would *you* miss most?"

"Pardon?"

I repeated the question and smiled as I heard Kyle frown. "I don't know," he answered at last. My question had disturbed him. "Matt told me that you see things with your other senses, though."

I didn't reply. Slowly I closed my book and waited.

"He said that you can taste shapes and hear colors," said Kyle.

Tasting shapes, hearing colors . . . Even to my ears, it sounded bizarre.

"Is that true?" he continued.

I shrugged. I'd have to have a serious word with Matt when I caught up with him. He wasn't meant to tell anyone about that. It wasn't even his secret to tell, it was my secret.

"I hope you don't mind me mentioning it," Kyle said

anxiously. "Matthew swore me to secrecy and he hasn't told anyone else—at least that's what he said."

"Why did he tell you?"

"We were talking and it slipped out," said Kyle. "I've never heard of anything like that before."

"It's called synesthesia. About ten people in every million have it, so don't go thinking I'm a fruit loop." I couldn't keep the edge out of my voice.

"I didn't think anything of the kind." Kyle laughed. "What's it like?"

"What's it like to see using your eyes?"

"It's . . . well, it's . . . it's a bit difficult to explain."

And I knew he'd got the point. "Exactly," I said. Then, wanting to change the subject, I asked, "So what d'you think of Belling Oak?"

"It's not bad, actually. It's a lot better than my old school. How come you don't come here with your brother?"

Instantly my face flamed, in spite of myself. I turned away, listening to the distant cheers and the shouting as the one-hundred-meter sprint race started.

"I was here for a while, but . . . there were problems," I said, still listening to the race.

"What sort of problems?"

I sighed. I'd say one thing for Kyle: he was persistent. "If you must know, the teachers spouted on and on about how it would be too dangerous for me, too hazardous, too nerve-wracking, how I'd be teased and bullied—stuff like that."

Kyle sniffed. "Sounds like excuses to me."

I turned to face him again. "It was. I already had friends here and Mum and I kept telling them that I was willing to put up with the rest, but they wouldn't have it. Then they started quoting health and safety regulations at us and they said it would cost too much to have the school converted so that I could find my way around without help. Plus the school's insurance company insisted that I left. So that was that."

"Were you very disappointed?"

"Course I was. I loved it here." I looked around, seeing it with my memory. All around me were the acres of grounds, divided by a trickling stream known as The Giggler because of the sound it made. I remembered how green the grass was, even in winter, and how in spring and early summer it was always covered in daisies. From the classroom windows the daisies looked like summer snow. And then there were the tall, sprawling oaks fringing the stream on both sides. The oaks had always been my favorite. They whispered amongst themselves, using the wind as cover. At one end of the upper field was the redbrick school building and way across on the other side, past the lower fields, were the tennis and netball courts. And the whole thing was so beautiful. I'd been to Belling for two years before I started to lose my sight. A whole two years to drink in the sights and sounds of the place before I got bounced out.

"So where d'you go now?"

"Aranden Hall."

"Never heard of it."

"It's a school for the blind. It's about twenty-five kilometers from here."

I turned back towards the sports field. I was seated near the stream, under the arms of one of the huge oak trees that gave Belling Oak its name. Every sports day, I always sat in the same spot. Far enough away from everyone else so that I wouldn't have to worry about being pushed over or swept aside by overly enthusiastic crowds, but close enough to hear what was going on. Some of my Belling friends thought it strange that I should want to sit by myself for most of the afternoon, but they were used to me by now. To be honest, I liked my own company. Besides, my friends made me remember . . . different times.

I forced my mind away from those thoughts and concentrated on the here and now. Matthew, my brother, was due to run in the next race—the two-hundred-meter, and the four-hundred-meter relay after that. He was bound to come last, as always, but he didn't mind and neither did anyone else. It would've been good to see him run, although my friends said he didn't so much run as plod frantically.

I had to take their word for it.

"I'm sorry if I asked too many questions," said Kyle. "I didn't mean to upset you."

"It's OK," I said. But I didn't deny that he'd upset me, because I couldn't. "Can I ask you something?"

I heard him nod, then catch himself and say, "Yeah! Sure!"

"Why're you over here? I mean, why aren't you with everyone else, watching the races?" *Please tell the truth. Please.*

"I saw you over here and I just wanted to say hello."

"I see." The heat from his lie swept over me like lava.

"Would you . . . er . . . I'm going for a burger after all the events are over. I don't suppose you'd like to come with me?"

Silence stretched between us like a piece of elastic.

"Yeah, OK," I said at last.

"Great! Great!" I would've laughed at the relief in his voice except that at that moment I didn't feel like laughing. For the life of me, I couldn't figure out why I'd said yes.

"Are you going to go back to your friends and watch the rest of the events?" I asked.

"No, I thought I'd stay here with you, if that's all right?"

"Sure. Let's go for a walk."

"A walk?"

"Around the grounds. Away from everyone else," I said.

"Can you . . . ? I mean, do you want . . . ?"

"I can walk, you know." I laughed. "It's my eyes that don't work, not my legs."

"Yeah, of course it is. Sorry." I heard Kyle get to his feet. I stood up, ignoring the hand he put out to help me.

"Let's walk downstream, then cross over the far bridge and walk around the tennis courts," I suggested.

"Fine."

We started walking. Kyle stuffed his hands in his pockets.

"So tell me what you can see," I said.

"Huh?"

"Describe what you can see." I smiled at Kyle. "Unless of course you'd rather not."

"No, I don't mind. I just . . . OK. Well, we're walking beside the stream now and there are oak trees on either side of the stream and way over there is the car park and over there is the school and . . ."

I put my hand on his arm. "That's not what I meant. Tell me what you can *see*."

"But I just did."

I gave him a hard look. "Kyle, have you got a scarf or a tie or something on you?"

"I've got my school tie on. Why?"

"Is it around your neck?"

"Yes."

"Take it off and put it around your eyes."

"Come again?"

"You heard right the first time," I said, laughing.

"Why d'you want me to do that?" Kyle's voice was wary, suspicious.

"I'm going to take you around the grounds."

"With my eyes blindfolded?"

I laughed at the panic in his voice. "That's right. You're going to have to trust me."

"But you . . . you can't see."

"So I've noticed," I teased. "So are you going to do it, or are you going to chicken out?"

Slowly Kyle removed the tie from around his neck and tied it around his eyes.

"You've got to do it so you can't see anything," I told him.

"I have."

"No, you haven't."

"How did you know . . . ?" Kyle was amazed. It was very gratifying. "OK! OK! My eyes are totally covered now."

"Let me touch your face," I said.

I heard him lean forward. I ran my fingers lightly over his face. My fingers began to hum again as I touched his skin. He had a large forehead and a strong nose and a firm chin and his lips were soft. I couldn't tell about his eyes because they were covered with his tie. His tie smelled of sweet green and sharp, tangy gold. Belling Oak colors. I would've been able to tell the colors even if I didn't already know what they were. Satisfied that his eyes were indeed covered, I linked his arm with my own. He instinctively stiffened at that.

"Don't worry, your friends won't be able to see us over here."

"It's not that," he lied. "But suppose we end up in the stream or something?"

"Then we'll get wet!"

There was a pause; then Kyle laughed. His body relaxing, he said, "All right, then. D'you know where you're going?"

"I know this school like the back of my hand. Don't worry," I assured him.

We walked for a minute, listening to the distant cheers and the occasional birdsong.

"What d'you think of that tree?"

"What tree?"

"The one right in front of us. It's my favorite of all the ones here," I said, adding, "No, don't," when I felt his other hand move upwards to remove the tie from around his eyes.

"But I can't see the tree. I can't see anything."

"See it without using your eyes," I told him.

"How do I do that?"

I took Kyle's hand and stretched it out in front of him until it touched the tree trunk. "What does it feel like?" I asked.

"Rough."

"What else?"

"Cool. Sharp in places. Here's a smooth bit."

"And what does it smell like?" I asked.

Kyle turned his head towards me.

"Go on!" I encouraged. "It's National Hug a Tree Trunk Day! Tell me what it smells like and feels like."

Reluctantly, Kyle moved in closer to the tree. He stretched out his arms to hold it. I could feel he felt very silly.

"It feels very strong. Like it could be here forever if it was left alone." Kyle's voice grew more and more quiet, but more and more confident. "And it's got secrets. It's seen a lot of things and knows a lot of things, but it's not telling. And it smells like . . . like rain and soil and a mixture of things."

"Come on," I said, taking his arm again.

"Where're we going?"

"To our next stop."

I led Kyle further down the stream before I turned us to our left and walked a few steps.

"Now you have to do exactly what I say," I told him, leading him down a gentle slope.

"Are we going to cross the stream here?" he asked, aghast.

"That's right." I smiled. "We're going to jump across."

"But . . . but I can't see where I'm going," Kyle protested.

"Then use your other senses. I'll help you."

"Why can't we use one of the bridges?"

"Because everyone does that. We're going to be adventurous." I grinned. "I want you to jump from here like a long-jumper. It's less than half a meter to the other side at this point. Just jump, then let your weight fall forward and grab hold of one of the tree roots sticking out of the ground. OK?"

No answer.

"OK, Kyle?"

"D'you really think this is a good idea?"

"You'll just have to trust me. Once you've grabbed the tree root, haul yourself up out of the way 'cause I'll be right behind you."

"OK," Kyle said dubiously.

I straightened him up and said, "Don't worry. My nan can jump half a meter and she's got bad knees—always assuming I've led us to the right bit of the stream, of course."

"You mean you're not sure?" Kyle was appalled.

"I'm only winding you up," I told him gleefully.

"You're enjoying this, aren't you?"

"You'd better believe it! Now then. After three. One . . . two . . ."

"Three—" Kyle shouted.

And he jumped.

To be honest, I was impressed. I didn't think he had it in him. I heard an "Ooof!" followed by the mad scramble of his hands as he sought and found a tree root. He hauled himself up the bank to the level ground beyond.

"Here I come," I shouted.

And I jumped. In a way, I'm sorry Kyle didn't see me. A sighted person couldn't have done it better. I landed cleanly, then stepped up the bank.

"Are you OK?" I asked.

"I think so."

I turned towards his voice. "How did it feel to jump?"

"I don't know," said Kyle.

"Yes, you do."

His sharp intake of breath told me that I was right. "I was . . . a bit nervous," he admitted. "I know the water is only a few centimeters deep, but it suddenly felt like it was kilometers deep and kilometers down."

"And how did you feel when you landed on the other side?"

"Relieved!"

"Anything else?"

"Yeah. Kind of proud of myself."

"Being blind," I began, "is like jumping off a cliff with the water below kilometers deep and kilometers down—except you jump never knowing what's on the other side of the cliff. Everything's an adventure for me. Walking along the street, going into a shop, meeting new people, even reading a book. I never know what I'll come across or what I'll find, whether I'll be delighted or disappointed, hurt or happy. Does that make sense?"

"I think so." Kyle didn't sound sure at all. But it was a start.

I reached out to link arms with him again. "Have you still got the tie around your eyes?"

"Yes."

"Then it's time for our next step."

I led the way along the fence towards the tennis courts.

"I have no idea where we are," Kyle said, perplexed.

"That's OK. I do."

We walked on for another few minutes before I stopped.

"Where are we now?" asked Kyle.

"What can you hear?" I asked.

He was still for a moment. "Birds and a faint whirring sound."

"That whirring is the traffic on the other side of the school building," I replied.

Kyle turned his head slightly. "I can hear some cheering now from the sports field, but it's very faint."

"Anything else?"

"I don't think so."

"OK. Kneel down."

"Why?"

"Trust me!"

"I wish you'd stop saying that!" Kyle's tone was dry, but he still knelt down.

I smelled what I was looking for. The scent was overwhelming. I took Kyle's hand and put it out to touch the thing I could smell.

"Just use your index finger and your thumb to touch this," I said.

When Kyle's fingers were on the object I let go of his hand.

"What is it?" he asked, his voice more than curious.

"What d'you think it is?" I asked.

"I don't know . . . ," Kyle said slowly. "It feels like a bit of velvet, but there wouldn't be velvet around the tennis courts."

I reached out and touched the object, my fingers next to Kyle's. "A deep yellow velvet."

"How can you tell what color it is?"

"Yellow has got quite a high voice. This yellow's voice is slightly lower, which means the shade is deeper, but it's definitely yellow," I told him.

"Do you know what it is I'm touching?" Kyle asked.

"Yes, I do." And all at once I didn't want to do this any more. I felt wistful and sad. "Take off your tie now. Have a look at what you're touching."

Kyle removed his tie at once and gasped. "It's . . . it's a flower . . . ," he said, shocked.

"Beautiful, isn't it?"

"A yellow flower," Kyle whispered.

"There's more to seeing than looking, Kyle," I told him. "Your eyes work. Never forget what a gift that is. I can taste light and feel colors and I'm grateful. But to *see* . . ."

"A flower . . ." Kyle's voice was awestruck. I didn't have his full attention. I wondered if he'd even heard me.

"Kyle, touching that flower and seeing it with your fingers—that's what seeing with my other senses is a tiny bit like. I see things in ways that you can't or won't because you don't have to. I'm grateful for that as well. Because I can still appreciate the things around me. Maybe even more than a lot of sighted people do."

I sensed Kyle looking at me then. Really looking—for the first time. I wondered how he saw me now. I smiled at him as he straightened up.

"I . . . look, I have something to tell you," Kyle began uneasily.

"Forget it."

"No, it's important. I . . ."

"Dean and Joseph bet you that you couldn't get me to go out for a burger with you. But just so you know, they've each asked me out and I turned them down flat, so they reckoned you had no chance."

Silence.

"Stop it! You're staring!" I laughed.

"How did you know that?"

"What? About the bet or that you were staring?"

"Both."

"'Cause I'm brilliant!" I teased. "And by the way, I wouldn't tell my brother about the bet if I were you. He's a bit overprotective where I'm concerned and he'd probably want to punch your lights out."

"I . . . I suppose you don't want anything more to do with me?"

"I knew about the bet before you'd even said one word to me—remember?"

"I still don't understand how."

"I heard you."

"But we were practically across the field," Kyle protested.

"No, you weren't. You were only several meters away and the wind was blowing in my direction."

When Kyle didn't answer I said, "Are you OK?"

"We'd better go back," he said, his tone strange.

Now it was my turn to be surprised. "What's the matter?"

It was a long time before Kyle answered. We started back to the sports field, my arm lightly resting on his. I knew the way back without any problems, but I had wanted to sense what he was feeling. And it didn't take a genius to guess from the way his muscles were stiff and tense what was going on in his head. He wasn't happy.

"Kyle?"

"I'm sorry, Amber. I guess you hate me now. And I don't

blame you. I behaved like a real jerk." The words came out in a rush of genuine embarrassment. And there was something else, something more, behind them.

"Why should I hate you?"

He looked at me then. And his eyes hadn't changed back—I could tell. He was still looking at me with the eyes of someone who could see *me*. Not a blind girl. Not someone to be pitied or patronized. Not someone who had less than him. But a girl who could see without using her eyes.

"So d'you still want to go out for a burger later?" Kyle's voice was barely above a whisper. If it wasn't for my bat ears I doubt if I would've heard him.

"Course. I'm starving."

There was no mistaking the sigh of relief that came from Kyle. It made me giggle.

"D'you know something?" Kyle stopped walking. He looked all around him, then straight at me. "I hadn't noticed before, but everything around me is . . ."

He shut up then. I could feel the self-conscious waves of heat radiating from him. I couldn't help it. I burst out laughing, which made Kyle even more self-conscious.

"Come on," I said. "Let's go and watch my brother come last in the four-hundred-meter relay."

And we walked over the bridge together to join the others.

Lois Lowry

Excerpt from

A SUMMER TO DIE

Molly is in the hospital again, and it's my fault.

Why can't I learn when to keep my mouth shut? I'd already said something I regretted, to Ben, and hadn't had the nerve to go to him and apologize. It was just a week later that I blew it with Molly.

She was lying on her bed, in her nightgown, even though it was eleven in the morning. She's gotten so darn lazy, and my parents don't even say anything to her about it. That's partly why I was mad at her, to begin with, because she was still in her nightgown at eleven in the morning.

She was grouchy and mad, too. I'm not sure why. I think mostly it was because school had just ended, before she'd even had a chance to go back. Tierney McGoldrick hardly ever calls her anymore. She doesn't know it, but toward the end of school he started dating a red-haired senior girl. At least I was smart enough not to tell Molly *that*.

But there she was, lying on her bed, grumbling about how awful she looks. I am so sick of hearing Molly talk about how she looks. Her face is too fat. Her hair is too thin. To hear her talk, you'd think she was really a mess, when the truth is that she's still a billion times prettier than I am, which is why I'm sick of listening to her.

I told her to shut up.

She told me to drop dead, and before I dropped dead, to pick up my sneakers from her side of the room.

I told her to pick them up herself.

She started to get up, I think to pick up my sneakers and throw them at me, and when she swung her legs over the side of the bed, I suddenly saw what they looked like.

"Molly!" I said, forgetting about the sneakers. "What's wrong with your *legs?*"

"What do you *mean*, what's wrong with my legs?" No one had ever criticized Molly's legs before; in fact, even I have to admit that Molly's got nice legs. She held up her nightgown and looked down.

Both of her legs were covered with dark red spots. It looked like a lot of mosquito bites, except that they weren't swollen.

"Does it hurt?"

"No," she said slowly, looking puzzled. "What could it be? It wasn't there yesterday, I know it wasn't."

117

"Well, it's there now, and it sure looks weird."

She pulled her nightgown down to cover her legs. Then she got into bed and pulled the covers up around her. "Don't tell anyone," she said.

"I will, too. I'm telling Mom." I started out of the room.

"Don't you *dare*," Molly ordered.

I'll be darned if I'll take orders from Molly. Anyway, I really thought my parents ought to know. I went downstairs and told Mom that there was something wrong with Molly's legs; she jumped up with a frightened look and went upstairs. I stayed out of it after that, but I listened.

I heard Mom and Molly arguing. I heard my mother get my father from the study. Then more arguing with Molly. I heard my mother go to the upstairs phone, make a call, and go back to Molly.

Then Molly crying. Yelling. I had never in my life heard Molly like that before. She was screaming, "No! I won't! I won't!"

Things quieted after a few minutes, and then my father came down. His face was very drawn, very tired. "We have to take Molly back to the hospital," he told me abruptly, and without waiting for me to answer, he went out to start the car.

Mom came downstairs with Molly. She was in her bathrobe and slippers, and she was sobbing. When they were by the front door, Molly saw me standing all alone in the living room. She turned to me, still crying, and said, "I hate you! I hate you!"

"Molly," I whispered, "please don't."

They were in the car and ready to leave when I heard my mother call to me. I went outside, letting the screen door bang behind me, and walked over to the car. "Molly wants to tell you something," Mom said.

Molly was in the back seat, huddled in the corner, rubbing her eyes with the back of her hand. "Meg," she said, choking a little because she was trying to stop crying, "tell Ben and Maria not to have the baby until I get home!"

"Okay." I nodded. "I'll tell them." As if they had any control over it! But I would tell them what Molly said, just because Molly asked me to. At that point I would have done anything in the world for Molly.

I went back upstairs, picked up my sneakers and put them in the closet. I made Molly's bed. The pussy willows were still there, in their little vase. The photographs of Will were back on the wall, and the two of Molly and her flowers were with them now. The chalk mark was still there, faded, but there. It was a nice room, except that an hour before, Molly had been in it, and now she wasn't, and it was my fault.

I went down to the darkroom, gathered up the photographs of Maria I'd been working on, and walked across the field to their house.

Will Banks was there, having lunch with Ben and Maria. They were all sitting outside at the picnic table, eating the entire crop of peas. There was a huge bowl of them in the middle of the table, and they were each eating from it with their own spoons, as if it were the most normal sort of lunch in the world.

"Hey, Meg!" Ben greeted me. "How's it going? Have a pea. Have *two* peas!"

He fed me two peas from his spoon; they were the tenderest, sweetest peas I've ever eaten. I sat down on the bench beside Will, and said, "Molly's back in the hospital, and she says please don't have the baby until she comes home. I know that's a dumb thing to say," and then I started to cry.

Will Banks put his arms around me and rocked me back and forth as if I were a baby. I cried until his shirt collar was wet clear through, saying "It's my fault, it's my fault, it's my fault" over and over again. Will said nothing except "There. There."

Finally I stopped crying, sat up straight, blew my nose on the handkerchief Will gave me, and told them what had happened. No one said very much. They told me, of course, that it wasn't my fault. I knew that already. Ben said, "You know, sometimes it's nice just to have someone to blame, even if it has to be yourself, even if it doesn't make sense."

We sat there quietly for a minute, and then I asked if I could borrow Maria's spoon. She wiped it on her napkin and gave it to me, and I ate all the peas that were left in the big bowl. There were *pounds* of peas, and I ate them all. I have never been so hungry in my life.

The three of them watched in amazement while I ate all those peas. When I was finished, Maria started to giggle.

Then we all started to laugh, and laughed until we were exhausted.

It is so good to have friends who understand how there is a time for crying and a time for laughing, and that sometimes the two are very close together.

I took out the photographs of Maria. Will had seen them, of course, because we'd worked on them together. He is as able in the darkroom now as I am, but our interests are different. He is fascinated by the technical aspects of photography: by the chemicals, and the inner workings of cameras. I don't care so much about those things. I care about the expressions on people's faces, the way the light falls onto them, and the way the shadows are in soft patterns and contrast.

We looked at the pictures together, and talked about them. Ben was much like Will, interested in the problems of exposure and film latitude; Maria was like me: she liked seeing how the shadows curved around the fullness of the baby inside her, how her hands rested on the roundness of her middle, how her eyes were both serene and excited at the same time.

"Meg," she said, "Ben and I were talking about something the other night, and we want you to think it over and talk about it with your parents. If you want to, and if they don't mind, we'd like you to photograph the birth of the baby."

I was floored. "Golly," I said slowly, "I don't know. It never occurred to me. I mean, I don't want to intrude."

But they were both shaking their heads. "No," Ben said. "It wouldn't be an intrusion. We wouldn't want just anyone there, and of course you'd have to be careful to stay out of the way and not to touch anything sterile. But you're special, Meg; you're close to us. Someday Maria and I would like to be able to look back at that moment. We'd like the baby, someday, to be able to see it, too. You're the one who can do it, if you want to."

I wanted to, desperately. But I had to be honest with them, also. "I've never seen a baby being born," I said. "I don't even know much about it."

"Neither have we!" Maria laughed. "But we'll prepare you for that part. Ben will show you our books, and explain everything in advance so that you'll know exactly what to expect when the time comes. Only, Ben," she added to him, "I think you'd better do it *soon,* because I don't know how much longer we have. The calendar says two weeks, but there are times when I wonder if it might be sooner."

I promised to talk to my parents, and Ben said he would, too. Suddenly I thought of something. "What if it's born at night?" I asked. "There won't be enough light. I could use a flash, I suppose, but—"

Ben held up one hand. "Don't worry!" he said. He cupped his hands into a megaphone and held them against Maria's stomach. Then he spoke to the baby through his hands: "Now hear this, kid. You are under instructions to wait until Molly comes home. Then come, but do it in daylight, you hear?

"That'll do it," Ben said. "Maria and I are determined to have an obedient child."

Before I left, I took Ben aside and spoke to him alone. "I'm sorry, Ben, for what I said that day."

He squeezed my shoulders. "That's okay, Meg. We all say things we're sorry for. But do you understand now what I was talking about that day?"

I shook my head and answered him seriously, honestly. "No. I think you're wrong, to anticipate bad things. And I don't understand why you even want to think about something like that. But I'm still sorry for what I said."

"Well," Ben said, "we're friends, anyway. Hang in there, Meg." And he shook my hand.

Will walked me home across the field. He was very quiet. Halfway home, he said, "Meg, you're very young. Do you think it's a good idea, really, being there when that child is born?"

"Why not?"

"It might be very frightening. Birth isn't an easy thing, you know."

"I know that." I dislodged a small rock with one toe and kicked it through a clump of tall grass. "For Pete's sake, Will, how can I learn if I don't take risks? You're the one who taught me that!"

Will stopped short and thought for a minute. "You're

absolutely right, Meg. Absolutely right." He looked a little sheepish.

I looked around the field. "Will, what happened to all those little yellow flowers that were here last month?"

"Gone until next June," he told me. "They've all been replaced by July's flowers. Molly's goldenrod will be in bloom before long."

"I *liked* those little yellow ones," I said grumpily.

" 'Margaret, are you grieving over Goldengrove unleaving?' " Will asked.

"What?" I was puzzled. He never called me Margaret; what was he talking about?

He smiled. "It's a poem by Hopkins. Your father would know it. 'It is the blight man was born for, It is Margaret you mourn for,' " he went on.

"Not me," I told him arrogantly. "I *never* mourn for myself."

"We all do, Meg," Will said. "We all do."

That was three weeks ago. July is almost over. Molly isn't home yet. The baby hasn't been born, so I suppose it's following Ben's instructions and waiting for her. I've studied the books on delivering babies with Maria and Ben, and I'm ready to do the photographs. My parents don't mind. When I asked them, they said "Sure" without even discussing it. They're very preoccupied. I know why, finally.

It was a few nights ago, after supper. My dad was smoking his pipe at the kitchen table. The dishes were done; Mom was sewing on the quilt, which is almost finished. I was just hanging around, talking too much, trying to make up for the quiet that had been consuming our house. I even turned the radio on; there was some rock music playing.

"Hey, Dad, dance with me!" I said, pulling at his arm. It was something silly we used to do sometimes, back in town. My dad is a *terrible* dancer, but sometimes he used to dance with Molly and me in the kitchen; it used to break my mother up.

He finally put down his pipe and got up and started dancing. Poor Dad; he hadn't gotten any better since the last time we did it, and I think I have, a little. But he's pretty uninhibited, and he tried. It was dark outside; we had eaten late. Mom turned on the light, and I could see on the kitchen walls some of the drawings of wild flowers that Molly had been doing, that she had hung here and there. Dad and I danced and danced until he was sweating and laughing. Mom was laughing, too.

Then the music changed, to a slow piece. Dad breathed a great sigh of relief and said, "Ah, my tempo. May I have the pleasure, my dear?" He held out his arms to me and I curled up inside them. We waltzed slowly around the kitchen like people in an old movie until the music ended. We stood facing each other at the end, and I said suddenly, "I wish Molly was here."

My mother made a small noise, and when I looked over at her, she was crying. I looked back at Dad in bewilderment, and there were tears on his face, too, the first time I had ever seen my father cry.

I reached out my arms to him, and we both held out our arms to Mom. She moved into them, and as the music started again, another slow, melancholy song from some past summer I couldn't remember, the three of us danced together. The wild flowers on the wall moved in a gradual blur through our circling and through my own tears. I held my arms tight around the two of them as we moved around in a kind of rhythm that kept us close, in an enclosure made of ourselves that kept the rest of the world away, as we danced and wept at the same time. I knew then what they hadn't wanted to tell me, and they knew that I knew, that Molly wouldn't be coming home again, that Molly was going to die.

Rosie Rushton

SKIN DEEP

"What do you mean, you aren't coming?" My sister stared at me incredulously. "You can't miss it—everyone goes to the End of Year Ball."

"So I'm breaking with tradition," I retorted. I would have smiled if I could, but I can't, which is half the problem.

"But Ellie," she pleaded, "you can't opt out. Like Matt was saying—"

"I'm not interested in what Matt or anyone else was saying!" I shouted. "Now just leave me alone, OK?"

After Jess had flounced out of the room, I felt a complete cow. I knew Jess had mentioned Matt because she thought it would make me change my mind, but in fact the opposite was true.

"Sorry, Ellie." Jessica poked her head round the door

two seconds later. I wasn't surprised—people do a lot of apologizing to me these days. "It's just that—well, everyone's rooting for you and remember what Mum said? You can't hide away forever. And besides, I need you there."

"Oh sure," I teased, trying to lighten the mood. Jess has been really good to me these last eleven months and I hate it when we fall out. "Like you're not going to be fully occupied with the Three Musketeers!" Or Four Musketeers, I thought to myself.

My sister—my not-in-the-least-bit-identical twin—is gorgeous. She has long, naturally blond hair, eyes the color of speedwells and tiny dimples in her cheeks and chin, which boys seem to find irresistible. Don't get me wrong—I used to look pretty OK too, in a chubby kind of way. My legs are my best assets—which is just as well considering what happened. But of course, I don't exactly attract the following that my sister manages. Currently, Jess has four guys salivating over her: Oliver—the class high-flyer, who is dark and sultry and up himself; Alex—who is fair and freckled and turns scarlet every time Jess flutters her eyelashes at him; and James—who's sweet and seems about three years younger than her. And then there's the one we don't mention, Matt. Who is—well, Matt.

We've known Matt since we were little kids at primary school. Our mum used to take him to school because his mother was often ill, and then, after she died, Matt used to spend hours round at our house in the holidays while his dad was at work.

He was more like a brother in those days, I guess—but suddenly that changed.

I think I fell in love with Matt when I was fourteen. You know how it is—one day he's just the guy next door, the next you find yourself dreaming about him, and hanging out of the window in the hope of seeing him in his rugby gear going off to practice. Then he asked me to go with him to the rugby club awards party—he was dead chuffed about it because he was getting an award for Most Improved Player.

Jess was not happy about it.

"We always do everything together," she asserted firmly. "You can't go without me—you won't talk to anyone."

I'd always been known as the shy one, largely because once Jess is on a roll, no one can get a word in edgeways.

"I'll be talking to Matt," I protested. Jess ignored me.

"Don't worry," she said bossily. "I'll find a way to get there."

And of course she did. Jess always finds a way to do what she wants. She started chatting up Ben Hardwick, who was one of Matt's best friends, and the next thing you know, she's coming to the party.

But it was OK, because Matt didn't leave my side all evening. We danced practically every dance and when we weren't dancing we sat and talked nonstop. He said I was pretty and witty (*West Side Story* was being reshown at our local cinema) and he made me feel a million dollars. That night, he kissed me; my first really proper, long, slow, smoochy kiss. I could see Jess watching me out of the corner of her eyes, and it was cool to see how surprised she looked.

After that, we were inseparable—Matt and me, not me and Jess. We would walk Matt's dog over the Downs and didn't have to say anything—we just held hands and drank in the views, and he didn't think it was boring like some of the guys I'd known.

But it wasn't all lovey-dovey stuff either: we talked for hours about everything from politics to rap music, and we laughed a lot.

We'd been together for six months when it happened. It was Saturday 25th July. Of course, everyone knows that date now—they call it 25/7. The day of our Town Carnival. It was a glorious, Technicolor summer day—the kind you get about once every three years in England. The papers said that made it worse, because there were even more people than usual. Everyone was in skimpy clothes, strolling about watching the jugglers and street musicians in the Market Place or lounging on the stone steps by the fountains, licking ice creams. I was on cloud nine because just before we left for the Carnival, Matt had gone all pink and shy and fumbled about in his pocket.

"I got you this," he said, thrusting a little box into my hands. "For a six months' anniversary present. You probably won't like it, and that's OK, you can change it, I mean, it's nothing really . . ."

By then I'd opened the box.

"It's beautiful," I murmured, not just because I wanted him to feel good, but because it really was—a tiny silver shell with a pearl in the middle, hanging on a fine silver chain.

"It's not expensive or anything," Matt apologized. "It's just from the market."

"No, it's from you," I said, and leaned forward so that he could fasten it round my neck. "I'll keep it forever."

Dumb thing to say.

Anyway, after that we headed for the Carnival. It had taken over the whole town center; streets were packed with waltzers, bouncy castles and dodgems; food stalls crammed the side roads and music blared out from loudspeakers. We met up with loads of our mates, ate ice cream and hot dogs and chips, and then felt sick riding the roller coasters.

When I think about what happened, it's as if there's a movie playing in slow motion in my head.

"Come on," Matt is saying again, "let's go on the Screamin' Spinner."

I remember the sick feeling in my stomach, remember the way I shook my head, said that I was dying of thirst and couldn't do another thing till I'd had a drink. I remember being afraid to say that I was terrified of fast roller coasters, because I knew Matt adored them and he'd once told me that he despised weedy girls who wouldn't have a laugh.

"Not me," I said as casually as I could. "I need a drink— I'm fried. You go."

"Not without you," he replied. "Tell you what, I'll keep our place in the queue—you go and get some Pepsi."

Then the pictures in my head fast-forward. I'm standing in line at the juice and cola bar outside Hendersons, I'm actually letting mums with little kids go ahead of me, because I reckon Matt will get to the front of the roller coaster queue and go on the ride without me. No way am I going spinning round at speed and turning upside down and disgracing myself by throwing up all over him.

And then, suddenly, that's just what I am doing. There are no pictures in my head after that. Just the noise of a deafening bang and then another, of screaming, the feeling of flying through the air, of searing, agonizing pain in my eyes, of a choking feeling in my throat, then a sickening, jarring thud. And I remember the Town Hall clock striking three.

I wish I could say that I don't remember any more, but I do. I remember lying there, choking as blood spurted from my nose and mouth, conscious of people running, jumping over me, shouting, "Bomb!" and crying. I remember trying to open my eyes, but they seemed stuck together. I remember struggling to lift my arm, shrieking in pain, to touch my face.

And I remember finding bare cheekbone.

The papers the next day reported that the paramedics had to abandon their ambulances and run down the street because all the rides and stalls were blocking the way. The guy who reached me just said, "Jesus," and whether it was the panic in his voice, or the loss of blood, I don't know. But at that point I passed out.

Teenager's face blown to pieces in Carnival bomb. That's what one of the more sensational tabloids had as its headline. *Surgeons dig two dozen shards of glass from 16-year-old's face.* There were before-and-after photos in the press, like they really wanted to rub salt into the wound. The before pictures showed me and Jess on the beach at Brighton; the after pictures concentrated on me, hair shorn to my scalp, in a clear plastic film I had to wear night and day. They were the last photos I have ever had taken. I refuse to go near a camera anymore.

I was lucky, I know that. Ten people died; two more lost arms or legs. But I feel like I lost me.

Matt came to see me in hospital. He didn't stay long. You can't blame him. I guess looking at me must have made him want to vomit, and anyway, I totally refused to look at him. Well, wouldn't you? I was a mess. He tried to get me to talk, but I just told him to go away. I couldn't bear to see him making such an effort to be nice when it was clear it was the last place he wanted to be.

I was in hospital for seven weeks. They took skin from my thighs to try to patch my face, they set my broken collarbone and arm and ankle and they gave me physio-therapy. At least three times a week Matt came in—and every time I told the nurses to send him away. One of them told me I was crazy to give the elbow to a guy as fit as Matt, but I knew she was just doing this "positive input" stuff you read about.

Eventually, they let me go home. I had to keep this cling-film stuff all over my cheeks and forehead while the burns healed. I was going to miss a year of school. Instead of lessons I had lots of rest, hospital appointments, sessions with the counselor. I didn't go out unless it was in the car. I just wanted to lock myself away because I looked so ugly, so tainted, so hideous. Some days, I even wanted to die.

After I got home, my best friends, Fran and Chloe, would call in to see me on their way back from school at least twice a week, but even that was hard. They would talk about the hockey team (I used to be goalie) and what they were doing in dance and drama, and how there was a new club opening down by the river and how we should all go. But when they said that last bit, they never looked right at me—it was like they knew the answer already.

Matt popped in every day after I got home, and every time I refused to see him. I would lock my bedroom door, turn my music as loud as I dared and cry. Or shout. Or thump my fist on the floor until my knuckles turned as red as my cheeks. Sometimes it was because I was angry with Matt—if he hadn't pressed me to go on the ride, I wouldn't have hung about by the drinks stand for so long and maybe

I'd have been out of the way. . . . Sometimes I was just angry with myself; the ride was at the top of the street and no one on it was hurt. If I hadn't been such a wimp . . .

A couple of times, when I didn't know he was in the kitchen talking to my mum, I'd appear at the door and he'd say dumb things like "It's not looking too bad now, honestly." One time when he'd gone on about how it would be better in no time, I just blew. I told him to cut the crap and face facts, and if he couldn't do that, then he'd better leave me alone.

So he did. Oh, he still called round, but that was only when he was picking Jess up for a party, or walking her to school. I told myself that I wasn't bothered—that I wasn't even that keen on him, really. Don't get me wrong—Jess was a star. She never talked about Matt and her, what they did or where they went. She made a point of filling me in on the days she went out with Oliver or Alex or James, but Matt she dismissed as "OK, I guess. He misses you, though—I know he does." But I knew she was just trying to make me feel better. That's why I said no to the End of Year Ball. I didn't want pity—not from her, not from anyone.

I began to suspect that Matt and Jess were more than just good friends and I was proved right this afternoon. I was looking out the window and I saw Matt giving Jess a hug. Not a little "Goodbye, nice to have seen you" hug, but a long "Please don't ever let go of me" hug. That's when I took the necklace off. I'd only recently been able to put it round my neck again, but I'd always had it with me—I'd worn it as a bracelet while my face mended. Well, I ripped the necklace off, actually, so violently that the chain broke. I almost cried—but then, anger took over. OK, so I'd said that I would keep it forever, but that was when I looked normal, when I was proper girlfriend material, when I deserved to have a love token. Not now. I went into the kitchen, opened the pedal bin and flung the necklace inside. Then I ran upstairs, slammed my bedroom door and cried like I'd never cried before.

Of course, once I managed to stop, I realized I was starving. That's what always happens with me—if I cry, or lose my temper, I end up with this overwhelming desire to stuff my face with chocolate or biscuits or ice cream. I used to fight it because I didn't want to get spots, but since that doesn't matter now, I decided to go and raid the fridge.

I thought I had the house to myself. Mum and Dad play bridge on Thursdays and clearly Jess was hanging out with Matt. I'd just spooned Toffee Crunch and pistachio ice cream into a bowl when the front door slammed.

"Fancy a milk shake?" I heard Jess ask.

"Cool." It was Matt. I froze. They were heading this way and my eyes were red and puffy. OK, I know—with a face like mine that was the least of my worries, but still . . .

I grabbed my bowl and nipped into the laundry room, quietly shutting the door behind me. With a bit of luck, they'd get their drinks and go.

I guess Jess must have chucked the empty milk carton at

Matt—anyway, all I heard was the clunk of the pedal bin and then Matt's voice.

"What the hell . . . ?"

"What's the matter?"

"This." Matt's voice was croaky. "The necklace I gave Ellie. She said she'd keep it forever."

"It must have broken," I heard Jess say. "Perhaps it fell off and Mum found it and didn't know . . ."

Her voice trailed off. Even Jess, whose imagination has won her prizes for creative writing, couldn't come up with a valid reason for a silver necklace that I had adored ending up among the carrot peelings.

"No point in trying any longer, then, is there?" Matt said. "I thought she wasn't talking to me because she was embarrassed about her face. I thought I could make her realize that I don't care what she looks like, I just want her. But she's clearly not interested. Well, you know—we've certainly talked about it enough, haven't we? But she's clearly just not interested. I feel like a total prat."

My heart was pounding in my ears. I couldn't believe what I was hearing! Half of me wanted to go into the kitchen and say sorry, the other half was dreading being found.

"She does like you, really she does," Jess ventured. "She's still getting over the bomb—you know that. She hasn't really wanted to talk to anyone. Mum said it would just take time. I guess she thought you'd lose interest and she wanted to ditch you first."

It felt as though someone had sent a thousand volts of

electricity through my body. She was right—that was it. I'd been hurting physically for so long that I couldn't bear to hurt any more. And clearly he would have dumped me in the end—that was obvious and . . .

"I don't get it," Matt shouted. "We always had such a great time together. I don't get why she doesn't even just want to hang out. I miss her sense of humor. I miss our conversations. She always made me feel good about myself. . . ." His voice went all shaky as if he was trying not to cry. "I just miss *her*."

I guess at that moment I should have opened the door and walked into his arms, begged his forgiveness and said that I'd been a fool. If this were a film, I bet that's what would happen just before the credits rolled.

But it's not and I didn't. I'm still in the laundry room and they're in the den. I don't know what will happen. I don't know how I'll explain the broken necklace to Matt and I certainly don't know how he'll react when I do say something.

But I keep thinking that, even though I'm scarred, and even though things will never be the same, Matt still wants me. I guess I've been so wrapped up in how I look, I hadn't realized that he was missing me for me—not my face. And now I realize that I was missing him, too.

I can't get my head around it yet, but I'm smiling for the first time in a long while. It still itches when I smile, but who cares? It's a lot better than the alternative.

Cathy Hopkins

JOHN LENNON SAID...

Don't look at me, don't look at me, I prayed as Mrs. Goodwin peered over her glasses at the class. "We've a lot to talk about in the next few weeks," she said. "I don't want any of you to feel pressurized, but I want to give it some attention now so that it doesn't come as a big panic later."

Pff. Too late, I thought, I am already in major panic mode. And I knew exactly what it was she wanted to talk about—it was all anybody had gone on about this term.

"I want you to think about your future. Your goals. Ambitions," continued Mrs. Goodwin as I wrote "bingo" and drew a star around it on the notepad in front of me. "What you want to be when you're older. Right. Anybody got any ideas?"

Inwardly I groaned. I'd been dreading this. See, I don't

know. Haven't a clue. Not the faintest. I'm fifteen—how am I supposed to know what I want to do with the rest of my life?

Mrs. Goodwin started to look around the class, so I put my head down and tried to become invisible. This is something that is hard to do when you've shot up to five foot nine while the rest of your classmates are normal heights of five foot four or five.

"Jessica?"

I knew. I knew it would be me she asked first. "Yes, Miss."

"Let's get the ball rolling. Any idea what you'd like to do?"

I could feel myself growing red as everyone turned to look at me.

Duh, I dunno, I thought as a million mad thoughts went through my mind. Drug dealer. Stripper. Dog washer. Ghostbuster. Nun. It always happens when I'm put on the spot. Some rebel part of me takes over and I have to bite my lip not to let it out.

"Don't know, Miss," I blurted, wishing that she'd choose someone else.

"No idea at all?"

I shook my head. "Mmff." Oh, great on the intelligent conversation, Jessica, I told myself. Mmff. What's that supposed to mean? Luckily Mrs. G moved on to Daniella Davey, who had her hand up and looked like she was bursting to tell us all her plans.

"Lifeguard, Miss," she said.

"Now that's an original one. And why do you want to be a lifeguard?

"So I can give fit boys the kiss of life, Miss."

Everyone cracked up apart from Mrs. G. She's such a tart, Daniella Davey, but she clearly has mad stuff in her head too. It must be something they put in the water here at school. Remind me not to drink any ever again.

"Anyone got any sensible suggestions?" asked Mrs. Goodwin, wearily looking round.

By now, half the class had their hands up.

"Writer," said Chris Shaw.

"Nurse," said Chloe Miller.

"Flight attendant," said Jocelyn Buck.

"TV presenter," said Rosie Moffat.

"Rich and famous," said Alison Ball (she's my mate) and everyone laughed again.

Seems like everyone knows what they want to do. Everyone but me.

When did they find out? How? Like, did it just happen one night while in the bath? Did a vision appear of St. Job, the patron saint of careers, who said, "Thou, O Chloe Miller, thou shalt be a nurse"? Whatever. Other people have clearly had signs. So why hasn't it happened to me? And why, all of a sudden, do I have to decide now? Everyone used to say, "Oh, don't grow up too fast, Jess, enjoy your youth," but now it's "What are you going to do with the rest of your life? Come on, girl, make up your mind." Like, excuse me, how am I supposed to know? I didn't come with a set of instructions for life.

"Excellent choices," said Mrs. Goodwin. "It'll be easier to choose your subjects for next year if you have at least some idea of what you want to do. But as I said earlier, no pressure."

Yeah, right. Thanks a mill, Mrs. G, I thought as we filed out to break. A-level subjects, university, jobs, it's all anyone seemed to be talking about.

On the way home, I gazed out through the bus window into the May afternoon and thought seriously about "What I Want to Do When I Grow Up."

As the bus slowed down at the traffic lights, I watched an old bag lady sitting with a tramp on the bench outside Thresher's Wine Shop. Cans of lager in hand, they looked like they hadn't a care in the world. Round the corner came a very smart-looking businessman. I could tell by the way he walked that he was uptight about something. Short, stiff steps. Furrowed brow. He was on his mobile phone. He looked at his watch, ran his hand through his hair, talked animatedly into his phone. Bag Lady nudged Tramp and they watched Smart Man like he was putting on a cabaret for them. The tramp held out his lager to Smart Man. It was curtly refused. Even from where I was sitting, I could see the veins in his temple throb. Not a happy bunny, I thought as the lights changed and the bus chugged off once more. He reminded me of my brother-in-law, Richard. He works in the City. He works six a.m. (to miss the traffic) to nine p.m. (to miss his kids). My sister Gracie says that sometimes she feels that he is working for a lifestyle that he never gets to enjoy. Maybe the bag lady has got it right. Out in the sunshine, having a good time. No responsibilities. No cares. No bed in winter either. Bet that's not a barrel of laughs.

Oh God. What do I want to do? Be free? Be secure? Be rich? Fulfilled? Help the poor? Help myself? Be what? What?

After supper, I decided to quiz *la famille:* Mum, Dad, Gran, brother, dog, cat. They live with me—one of them ought to know what I'm capable of.

Boris, the Labrador, tried to answer when I asked him. He barked his head off and I cursed the fact that I don't speak Labradorese. I know he was trying to tell me something.

Duchess, the cat, did her usual Zen thing, which is to look deeply into my eyes and purr loudly. Luckily we have a telepathic connection.

"I know, I know. Be here now." I nodded at her. "I get it. Chill. Trouble is, I can't. I have to make decisions."

Her response was to turn her back on me in disdain. She does that when she thinks I'm not taking her seriously.

Mark, my elder brother, got up from the supper table and started mincing up and down with his hand on his hip.

"Be a *mo-dèle*," he said in a girlie voice. "Isn't that what all you stupid girls want to be? You've got the long blond hair, the long legs, you look OK if you make an effort and if you had plastic surgery to give you boobs, someone might employ you."

I flicked a forkful of mashed potato at him, which hit him square in the eye. Note for list of things that I'm good at: marksmanship. I could be a hit woman. Or a female James Bond. Death by mashed potato could be my speciality.

Mark sat back down and was loading up his fork ready to fire back when Mum passed by behind him and whipped it out of his hand.

"But she started it," Mark began to whine, but Mum gave him the evil eye.

"Oh, grow up, for heaven's sake, Mark," she said.

Heh, heh. I do love it when he gets blamed for something I did.

"So what ideas have you got so far?" asked Mum, sitting down opposite me.

"Nothing," I said.

"You used to want to be a vet," said Mum.

"Too much blood involved. Gone off that idea. You have to put animals down. Couldn't do it. What would you like me to do?"

Mum patted my hand. "Whatever makes you happy, love. That's what's most important to me."

Whatever makes me happy? Hmmm. In that case, I'll

stay at home, then. Get up at eleven. Hang out at the mall with my mates, lie on the sofa watching MTV and eating chocs, sponge off my parents and never work at all.

"Be a reality show celeb," said Mark.

"Like that's a career choice," replied Mum.

"It is," said Mark. "All you have to do is eat bugs or slugs in a remote jungle someplace or get locked up in a house for a few weeks with a bunch of nutters or have a big boob job and marry a footballer and you could be set for life."

"I don't think you're being very helpful, Mark," said Mum.

"Yeah, you can leave the table now," I added. "Go and do your homework like a good little sixth former."

Mark skulked off, but I added reality show celeb and footballer's wife to my list. Not bad ideas at all.

"What do you think, Dad?" I asked.

Dad looked up from his supper. "You've got a good brain, Jessica. I hope you'll use it."

"Yeah, but to do what?"

"Do as your mother and I do. Teach."

"No way."

"OK, so think about your best subjects," he asked.

I shrugged. "English. Art."

"OK, now think about your worst subjects."

"Maths."

"So there's a start. Don't do accounting."

"I think she should be a dancer," said Gran, getting up to take her plate to the sink. "You're a lovely mover, Jessica."

And she began to waltz round the kitchen with some unseen partner. I thought it was supposed to be young kids who had imaginary friends. Not in this house. Gran has a gang of them in every room.

As the family settled down to watch the soaps, they lost interest in My Great Dilemma, so I decided to try Aunt Em, who lives two doors down the road. She sometimes has a different angle on things and luckily she was in, wasn't watching the soaps and was up for discussing the matter at hand.

"I didn't know what I wanted to do until I was thirty-five," she said. "I left school, traveled the Far East, taught meditation, sang in a rock-and-roll band, taught art in a mental hospital, studied astrology, worked as a masseuse, worked as a journalist, sold books in a friend's shop, was a cook in a health store for a while and now I make jewelry. So what does that make me?"

Good question, I thought as I glanced over her usual bohemian appearance and spiked up henna-ed hair. Experienced. Interesting. Slightly batty.

"I don't think your job should define who you are," said Aunt Em. "You meet so many people that identify so closely with what they do that it's hard to get beyond it to who they are as people."

"You mean, like Bill Newman," I said.

Aunt Em nodded. Bill lives at the end of the street. He's a politician. He looks like a politician. He introduces himself as Bill Newman, MP for Leighton South. As if MP for Leighton South is part of his surname. I think he was born with *I will be a politician* tattooed on his botty. People like him seem to know what they want to be from Day One. As if they're born grown up and responsible. Not me.

Aunt Em offered to read the tarot cards. At the end of the reading I got the Death card. It was in the position that is supposed to show what the future holds. Oh great, I thought. Now I needn't decide what I want to do when I grow up because I'm not going to grow up. But then Aunt Em told me that actually it didn't mean what I thought. The Death card actually means a new beginning—a new chapter. I couldn't help wondering why, in that case, it isn't called the New Chapter card. Anyway, in the end, the reading wasn't very helpful. It just said that I had a new chapter coming. And I already knew that. Maybe I should redesign the tarot card pack. I'm good at art and it would be a fun job. I'll add designer to the list, which so far reads: female James Bond, footballer's wife (but must get boobs as well as school-leaving exam scores) and card designer.

Just to be on the safe side, we checked the I Ching. It said something about no harm in waiting and then something else about crossing the Great Water. It always says something about the Great Water. If you're not already crossing it, you're about to. A bit like PMS, I thought. Since I had started my periods, it seemed that I was either having a period, was premenstrual or was postmenstrual.

There was no letup from hormone hell; no time off for good behavior. As the country-and-western song goes: Sometimes it's hard to be a wombat.

I'm not going to get the answers I need from fortune-telling, I thought as I left Aunt Em's house to go home. Unless what the cards and I Ching were trying to tell me was that I should be a fortune-teller. Or maybe a sailor with all that talk about crossing the water? Yeah. Maybe I should join the navy. Add it to the list.

When I got home, I wrote down all the things I am good at:

- Art.
- English.
- Debating.
- Sciences. Yeah. I'm OK at them, but don't know if I want to do a job in science.
- History. I get good marks but not sure I want to do anymore.
- Not maths. Not maths. Not maths. At least that's one thing decided.
- Snogging Josh Ryan (my boyfriend). He's so cool. Says I'm the best kisser he's ever been with. Maybe I could be a professional snogger. Teach it as an art.

I added that to the list. Snog teacher. Mrs. G was going to be well impressed with my *fabuloise* options.

* * *

Over the next few days at school, I talked to careers advisers. They were in most mornings, armed with brochures for college courses, talking to everyone in our year. Doctor, lawyer, teacher, nurse, media studies, business studies, endless choices. I couldn't sleep at night as a hundred job options swirled through my head.

I bit my nails down to the fingers.

I had bags under my eyes.

A spot was forming on my nose.

So much for the happiest days of my life. It was all too difficult. I so wished that there was something I could do. Some way I could opt out . . .

Of course, I thought as a brilliant idea popped into my head one night after supper. I immediately picked up the phone to call Josh.

"Hey, bug face," I said. "I think I know what I want to be."

"Hey, yourself. So shoot."

"A pregnant single mother."

"OK. Interesting one," said Josh, and I could hear him laughing softly at the other end of the phone.

"I'm not kidding. I was reading about it in Mum's paper at the weekend. You get an allowance and housing and clothing for you and the kid."

"Cool. I'll come right over and help you get started," he said. He was still laughing.

"OK. So you'd support me?"

"No way. But I am more than willing to be there for the fun part. The start. The sex. But after that, count me out. No, while you are wiping baby's bum and snot from his nose and trying to lose your pregnancy flab-a-dab and weeping because you have no social life, I will be away at university having a fab time misbehaving and meeting lots of young academic babe–types who will worship the ground I walk on. When you snivel past me during the uni hols with said snotty baby in pram, I will blank you, then go back to my groovy digs and write poetry about how I almost got caught by a fifteen-year-old tall blond looker. But didn't."

"Love you too, babe."

"It's your choice," he said. "But anytime you want an irresponsible seventeen-year-old to father your children, then leave you pregnant and penniless, I'm your man."

"Yeah, right. Thanks for taking me so seriously, Josh. I know I can always count on you."

"Anytime."

I wasn't serious either. Grainia Riley did the young single mum thing last year and I saw her in the park last week. She looked tired and sad. Although the housewife-mother thing might be an option way down the line, I am soooo not ready yet.

So what should I do? All my mates knew. Why not me?

My "I'm going to be rich and famous" friend Allie (who knows exactly what she wants to be—a journalist) called at seven and suggested that we take a stroll down to the job center to look in the window and on the way name as many jobs as we could.

"Hairdresser, shop assistant, bank manager, zebra-crossing person . . . ," said Allie as she flicked her long dark hair back once we got to the High Street and she saw that she had an audience. A guy on a bike almost rode into a lamppost as soon as he saw her. Men always react like that when they see Allie. She has the X-factor. That and very short skirts.

"Ambulance driver," I said as an ambulance whizzed past, sirens blasting.

We both said, *"Mo-dèle,"* and minced *à la* catwalk for a few yards as we went past a clothes shop with dummies in the window (hips thrust forward, bottom lip pushed out, sullen expression and then you glide, dahling, glide . . .) "Nurse, optician, fashion designer . . ."

"Hey, you know what, Jess?"

"What, Allie?"

"I think you're thinking about this in, like, totally the wrong way."

"OK. So what's the right way?"

"I'll tell you," she said. "See. You're thinking, like, all this choice you have is a curse . . ."

"Well, it is."

"No. It isn't. It's a blessing. Don't you see? You . . . *you* could do any of these things. Don't you see? You are pretty, tall—yes, maybe you could be a *mo-dèle*. . . ."

Cue more silly catwalk gliding.

"Seriously," Allie continued. "You're good at art. You're good at English. You're OK at science. You can get by in all your subjects. Don't you see? You could be a doctor, you could be a dancer. You could be both. Or neither. You have choice. Choice. We both do."

"Duh. That's what has been driving me batty for the last week, you dingbat. I've got to plan my future."

"You know what Mr. McNelly said in religious education the other day?"

"Oh no, you aren't going to go all holy moly on me, are you?"

Allie slapped me lightly. "No. Listen, you ignorant peasant. Listen. No. He was quoting John Lennon. He said that life is what happens to you when you're busy making other plans."

"Meaning?"

"OK, make a few plans, but be prepared to let them go if things change. You don't have to decide right now what career you're going to do. If you don't know, then you don't know, and that's where you're at. Notknowingness. Accept that. Yeah, you have to pick some subjects to study for A-levels. So do that. Pick the subjects you are interested in. You can always change courses if you're not happy. And maybe when you leave school, the way will become clearer. If not, take a gap year. But for the present, act on what you know now. And if you do get the wrong A-levels for what you eventually want to do, well, you can take the right ones at night school later—plenty of people do. Nothing is set in stone forever and ever, amen. It's true. Some people can't decide what they're going to be for the rest of their life at our age. You're one of them. You don't know at this very minute. But who knows what's going to happen? Or what life is going to throw at you while you're busy making plans? Things are changing all the time and stop looking at me like that. . . ."

"Well, you've come over all Wise Woman of Wonga."

"That's me," she said with a laugh. "Wise and really rather wonderful, don'tcha think?"

I laughed with her. I liked what she said and what John Lennon had said too. It was true. I thought about my sister. All through school she was adamant about being a lawyer. Earning megabucks. Expensive hols. No kids. Now look at her. Not even twenty-five and she's at home with twins. Our next-door neighbor, Robin. He was in telesales. He *was* Mr. Salesperson. Lived for his job. He was made redundant a couple of years ago. Now he does garden design and has never been happier. My uncle Martin was a successful photographer for years. Now with digicams and photo libraries on the Net, no one will pay the fees he used to get. He's gone into property with his wife. They buy up old places, do them up, sell them on. He never dreamed in a million years that he'd end up doing that. Mary Jacobs, two roads over, used to work as a cleaner. She won the lottery and moved to Barbados. Katie Palmer Smythe was married to a rich executive and had an affair. Husband found out, they had a messy divorce, now she works as a cleaner. Has Mary Jacobs's job, in fact. She never saw that coming.

Yeah. Allie was right. John Lennon too. Life is what happens when you're busy making plans.

The following day when Mrs. Goodwin cast her beady eyes over the class, I was ready for her.

"Now, Jessica. Have you thought any more about what you want to do when you leave school?"

"Yes I have, Miss."

"And?"

"Still don't know."

"Still don't know?"

"No, Miss."

And this time, it felt OK to admit it. Yes, I'd pick my subjects for next year. Not maths. Definitely English. And art. And later, well, who knows what job I'll do. I'm not totally sure just yet what, but one thing I do know and that is whatever happens, whatever changes along the way, I will always have choice. And that's not a curse, it's a blessing.

ABOUT THE AUTHORS

Lois Lowry is an award-winning author who has written many popular books for children and young adults, from her first novel, *A Summer to Die*, through the Anastasia Krupnik series, to her most recent novel, *Gossamer*. A two-time recipient of the Newbery Medal, for *Number the Stars* and for *The Giver*, Lois Lowry conveys through her writing her passionate awareness that we live intertwined on this planet and that our future depends upon our caring more and doing more for one another. Born in Honolulu, Lois Lowry has lived all over the world and now divides her time between Cambridge, Massachusetts, and Maine.

Meg Rosoff was born in Boston and had three or four careers in publishing and advertising before moving to London in 1989. Her phenomenal first novel, *How I Live Now*, won several awards in the United States and Europe, among them the Michael L. Printz Award and the *Guardian* Award for Children's Fiction. Her second novel is *Just in Case*. Meg Rosoff lives in London with her husband and their daughter.

Meg Cabot is the author of many books for young readers and adults, including the phenomenally successful Princess Diaries series, *All-American Girl*, *Teen Idol*, and *How to Be Popular*. When she is not reliving the horrors of her high school experience through her fiction, Meg divides her time between New York City and Key West with her husband and their one-eyed cat, Henrietta.

Melvin Burgess has written several highly acclaimed books for young readers, including *Smack*, which won the Carnegie Medal and the *Guardian* Children's Fiction Prize in England; *Lady: My Life as a Bitch*; and *Doing It*, winner of the *Los Angeles Times* Book Prize for Young Adult Fiction. He lives in Manchester, England, with his two children.

Anne Fine is a former Children's Laureate of England and a two-time winner of both of England's highest literary awards, the Carnegie Medal and the Whitbread Children's Book of the Year. She has written many highly acclaimed books for young readers, including *Up on Cloud Nine*; *Alias Madame Doubtfire*, on which the Robin Williams movie hit *Mrs. Doubtfire* was based; *Flour Babies*; *The Tulip Touch*;

and *Bad Dreams*. The mother of two daughters, Anne Fine lives in County Durham, England.

Sue Limb lives on an organic farm in a remote part of Gloucestershire. Her writing career has included various assignments for magazines and newspapers, radio work, television series, and several novels for adults published in Britain. Her books for children include *Big and Little*, *China Lee*, *Me Jane*, *Big Trouble*, *Mr. Loopy and Mrs. Snoopy*, and *Come Back, Grandma*, which was short-listed for the Smarties Prize. Her novels about the charmingly crazed Jess Jordan, who is featured in her story "You're a Legend," include *Girl, 15, Charming but Insane*; *Girl, Nearly 16: Absolute Torture*; and *Girl, Going on 17: Pants on Fire*, and are available from Delacorte Press. Sue Limb is quite interested in gardening, travel, green politics, agriculture, and rare breeds of poultry, about which she is particularly mad.

Jacqueline Wilson has written more than eighty-five books for young readers of all ages. In England, her *Double Act* won both the Children's Book of the Year Award and the Smarties Prize. Jacqueline Wilson also won the Children's Book Award for *The Suitcase Kid*, *Girls in Tears*, and *The Illustrated Mum* and has been short-listed five times and runner-up twice for the prestigious Carnegie Medal. She was named Children's Laureate for 2005 through 2007. Jacqueline Wilson lives near London in a small house crammed with fifteen thousand books.

Celia Rees was born and brought up in Solihull, England, and taught English in city comprehensive schools for seventeen years. She now spends her time writing, talking to readers in schools and libraries, tutoring creative writing students, and reviewing. She writes for children and teenagers. Her first book was published in 1993. Since then she has written many more novels and a number of short stories. Her novels have been translated into twenty-seven different languages and include *Witch Child*, *Sorceress*, and *Pirates!*, all of which were short-listed for major awards, both in Britain and abroad. Celia Rees lives in Leamington Spa, England, with her husband. She has a grown-up daughter, Catrin, who lives in London.

Malorie Blackman was a computer programmer before her first book was published in 1990. Since then she has had more than fifty books published, including the Naughts and Crosses trilogy (published in the United States by Simon and Schuster and winner of the FCBG Children's Book Award 2002 in Britain), *Pig Heart Boy* (which was short-listed for the Carnegie Medal in Britain and also won a BAFTA for Best Children's Drama), *Thief!*, and *Hacker*. When Malorie is not writing, she loves to read, watch films, and play computer games. More information can be found on her Web site, www.malorieblackman.com.

Rosie Rushton has written more than thirty novels for teens and young adults, including the Fab Five series, which is very popular in the United States; the What a Week series; and some very successful novels for older teens, her favorites being *Waving, Not Drowning; Tell Me I'm OK Really;* and *Last Seen Wearing Trainers*. She lives in Northamptonshire, in the middle of England, which is odd for someone who loves the sea. She is passionately interested in the lives and loves, as well as the angst, of teenagers and gets much of her inspiration from the young people she meets in her roles as a school governor, a grandmother, and a lay minister in the Church of England. She knows a book is working out well when her characters start refusing to do as she tells them—something that happens with alarming regularity. Her interests include researching her family tree, playing with her grandchildren, traveling, sharing good food with friends, and reading.

Cathy Hopkins lives in London with her husband and four cats, Molly, Maisie, Emmylou, and Otis. She spends most of her time locked in a shed at the bottom of the garden pretending to write books but is actually in there listening to music, hippie dancing, and talking to her friends on e-mail. Apart from that, she is looking for the answers to why we're here, where we've come from, and what it's all about. She is also looking for the perfect hairdresser. So far she has had forty-two books published, including the Mates, Dates series for teens, which has been published in twenty-three countries, including the United States, where the series has sold more than a million copies.